THE
WRITER'S
SOURCE
BOOK

Chris Sykes

Teach Yourself®

The Writer's Source Book

Inspirational ideas for your creative writing

Chris Sykes

First published in Great Britain in 2011 by Hodder Education. An Hachette UK company.

First published in US in 2011 by The McGraw-Hill Companies, Inc.

This edition published in 2019 by John Murray Learning

British Library Cataloguing in Publication Data: a catalogue record for this title is available from the British Library.

Library of Congress Catalog Card Number: on file.

Paperback ISBN 9781473688476

Ebook ISBN 9781473688483

1

The publisher has used its best endeavours to ensure that any website addresses referred to in this book are correct and active at the time of going to press. However, the publisher and the author have no responsibility for the websites and can make no guarantee that a site will remain live or that the content will remain relevant, decent or appropriate.

The publisher has made every effort to mark as such all words which it believes to be trademarks. The publisher should also like to make it clear that the presence of a word in the book, whether marked or unmarked, in no way affects its legal status as a trademark.

Every reasonable effort has been made by the publisher to trace the copyright holders of material in this book. Any errors or omissions should be notified in writing to the publisher, who will endeavour to rectify the situation for any reprints and future editions.

Cover image © Shutterstock.com

Typeset by Cenveo® Publisher Services.

Printed and bound in Great Britain by CPI Group (UK) Ltd., Croydon, CR0 4YY.

John Murray Learning policy is to use papers that are natural, renewable and recyclable products and made from wood grown in sustainable forests. The logging and manufacturing processes are expected to conform to the environmental regulations of the country of origin.

Carmelite House

50 Victoria Embankment

London EC4Y 0DZ

www.hodder.co.uk

Also available as an ebook

To my students, from whom I have learned much.

Acknowledgements

I would like to thank my wife, Siobhan, for her unfailing help and support to me at all times. And also to thank both Siobhan and Paula Jhung for reading and making very helpful comments on earlier drafts of the manuscript. Finally I would like to thank Victoria Roddam from John Murray Learning for asking me to write the book in the first place.

Contents

In one minute

What if you had always wanted to write?

What if you took a writing course?

What if you gained confidence writing and presenting your work in class?

What if your teacher told you to send off a few stories to magazines?

What if your work was rejected?

What if you started a novel or a script?

What if the writing started off well but then got harder so you gave up?

What if you started another novel or script?

What if you finished it and sent it off to a publisher, production company or agent?

What if the first one said no?

What if you sent it off again and again and they all said no?

What if they gave you little or no feedback so you did not know what was wrong with it?

What if you felt like giving up?

What if you found a book that did not pretend to have all the answers but promised to get you to start thinking about asking some of the right questions?

What if this book gave you some writing exercises to get you going?

What if this book gave you well-known examples to study and learn from?

What if this book helped you polish your writing to focus it more and make it more exciting?

What if this book helped you think about your characters and plotting in a new way?

What if you bought this book...?

1

Starting at chapter one

In this chapter you will learn:

- how to read and watch
- about targeting the reader
- games for characters
- strategies to stay in the creative bubble.

Reading and watching

When you read a book or see a movie or play, what do you remember most, the plot or the characters? When you are so excited by something you have just read or seen and can hardly wait to tell your friends, do you describe the plot twists or the intriguing characters? What stays in your mind?

In the 1989 film *When Harry Met Sally*, probably what most of us remember is the scene in the diner when the Meg Ryan character fakes an orgasm while eating. For her character to do something like that in the middle of a diner is unexpected. She is such a straight-laced character that there is a wonderful irony in seeing and hearing her do all this in public. The scene works because of the way she does it and because of the reaction of the Billy Crystal character, who is also surprised to hear these sounds come out of her mouth while eating, and in such a public place. This is a character-based scene beautifully acted by two consummate performers. The scene is fundamentally very well written. It is funny: it finishes with a memorable one liner from a watching female diner, and it is just about the right length for retelling. But what is happening in the plot is less important at that stage than the characters.

A story like *When Harry Met Sally* or an action story, like a James Bond or Indiana Jones movie, will elicit different responses. And what we each remember about a work we've read or watched probably depends on what sort of story it is. It probably also depends on us – on what we like about a story, whether it is plot or character – but think about it next time it happens to you and see what stays in your mind.

 ## Key Idea

A useful test is to ask yourself what you enjoy reading and viewing: the answers will be excellent indicators of what you should write.

So which comes first when you are writing – character or plot? Different writers will answer differently. For some it will be character; for others they will need the structure of the plot. If you were to ask readers and viewers what was more *important*, character or plot, as with politics you would probably get them voting different ways. Some people find plotting boring; probably because they don't have the mind for it. Whether you rate character or plot depends on what you read books or watch films for. It might also depend on memory: the ability to remember complicated plot twists and developments is not given to all of us and if you have ever tried to recount the plot of a book or film to someone, you will know how easy it is to get confused and be confusing.

Targeting the reader – how and why?

Some people argue that men read books and watch movies for action plots and women for character. This would be to argue that the kind of books we read and films we enjoy can be divided by gender. There may be something in it. Advertisers are not stupid and they certainly have a gender divide in mind when they schedule adverts on television, believing quite clearly that men and women enjoy different types of television programmes and films. Next time you are watching television, make a note of the advertisements that appear in the breaks or between programmes. You will find that companies pay to run adverts for 'feminine hygiene' products or make-up during a Jane Austen adaptation or a romantic comedy, presumably because they believe women, their target audience, will be watching. Advertisers pay vast sums of money to show adverts for cars or shaving during sports like the NFL Super Bowl or a Formula 1 Grand Prix because they know their target audience, men, will be watching, or women who might want to buy such products for their men. Maybe men and women do read and watch different books and films. If that is so, it is useful knowledge. Use it in your writing. But now we have mentioned advertising, and without going deeply into the entire gender argument, what we can learn from the world of marketing is that both knowing what we are writing and who we are writing for are important.

Key Idea

Know your audience. Don't think that 'selling' is anathema to writing. Writing has to be bought and it has to be sold. It is sold by the writer to the publisher or producer and by publishers and producers to the audience.

Publishers seek to manipulate readers to buy and read books (at least to buy them) and film companies seek to manipulate audiences to spend money seeing their films. The marketing budget for some Hollywood films is colossal: as much as they can afford and more. Writers, too, can and must market themselves today, though that is not new. Writers are not unfamiliar with marketing and manipulation. Writers themselves have been manipulators since stories first began to be told and they have always manipulated right there on the page and on the screen. Dickens is often associated with the remark 'make 'em laugh, make 'em cry and make 'em wait'. In fact Willkie Collins is probably the source, but these two friends were both talented artists who knew the art of manipulation. They were writers.

 Key Idea

Plotting is one of the most manipulative elements a writer can use. Taking an audience through a rollercoaster of tension and release is pure manipulation and readers love it.

We have drawn an analogy with advertising because advertising is not accidental; it can't afford to be. It is highly focused and targeted; it can't afford not to be. Similarly, writing is not accidental; it can't afford to be. It is highly focused and targeted; it can't afford not to be. At least this is true *of the end product*. As we will see through this book, in the actual writing, there are many ways to play with characters by putting them into situations to see what will happen. You can play with all the elements of writing while you are actually writing it. But at some point you have to rein the free writing in, you have to form and shape it; you have to give your writing form and focus.

 Key Idea

A book should be focused, but the writing we do to get there can be free and creative and exploratory.

In this book we shall look at both aspects of writing – the bringing into being and the shaping – as we explore the nature of character and plot and their relationship to each other. We will keep in mind the question of whether it is character or plot that is most important to a story. As for which comes first, character or plot, let's find out by going straight away into some brief exercises on character.

Games for characters

Anything might start you off. Anything might constitute the beginning of the process you go through to find a character, so here are some exercises that could help. Approach all the exercises in this book with an open mind – anything can come from them and frequently does.

Workshop: Alphabet soup

- Take a piece of paper and a pen.
- Write down all 26 letters of the alphabet in a random order in a single line across the top of the page. Make sure you don't miss any letters out. You should end up with a line something like this:

M Z Y S T U A C Q D E R L F H G I K X P V N B J W O

or:

V L J B D I Q T W Z F C A G K M R X Y U S P O E H N

- Now make up a sentence or two in 26 words using each new letter to start each new word. Do not change the order of the letters and use only these letters to start each word.
- Your sentence has to follow the pattern dictated by the letter – in the first example, start by writing a word beginning with the letter M, then Z and so on.
- It should be 26 words long.

Here is an example just typed out from the first list of words above without giving it much thought.

> *Mario Zanetti yearned sideways towards Utrillo Alsace calling quiz decisions every random laughing hour. Gianni instinctively kissed X-rays previously volunteered nobly by Juliette weeping oceans.*

This is a strange world isn't it? Complete nonsense of course, but who said it had to make sense? The important thing here is not to censor yourself. It is just fun. Who cares what comes out? Do it and have a laugh.

On the other hand there might be something going on in the writing that could be played with and developed further. We have at least three potential characters here. We don't know much about Utrillo Alsace apart from the name, but what of Juliette 'weeping oceans' while she nobly volunteered her X-rays? And there is Gianni instinctively kissing her X-rays. What is suggested to us about their characters and their relationship? And what is suggested too by the accident of 'every random laughing hour'. No writer would come up with that sentence if they had not been playing a game like this, but it has potential for being part of something interesting. It is not hard to imagine it as a line in a poem, or you could take it as the start of a further piece of writing.

 ## Write

Write the phrase 'every random laughing hour' at the top of a piece of paper. Set a timer for five minutes and, keeping the phrase in mind, write freely for the whole five minutes. Just write and see what comes. Have fun.

This type of game works well in a writing class. Writing students can have a lot of fun creating surprising and exciting snatches of images and ideas. It is also possible to do this quietly at home by yourself, stuck at your desk one morning, not knowing what you are going to write.

It may have absolutely nothing to do with anything you want to write but it may help to kickstart you. A game like this might well start you off on a character or a situation, or it might do nothing more than get the vocabulary working, put you in touch with language and test you a little to search for words. It is a sort of limbering up like athletes and dancers do: a limbering up for the mind and the tongue.

Exercises like this are a good way to limber up. They get us into the place where we can produce exciting, new and different writing; a place away from the controlling, rational, reasonable, logical mind; a place where we can tap into our reserves of language and also our intuition; where words and ideas can come and surprise and delight us. We often have to trick our conscious, logical and controlling mind into playing because it is from play that creativity can come.

Key Idea

If you are stuck with knowing how to start a piece of writing, try a word game. Have fun, play and see what creative play unlocks.

 ## Write

Write down your own list of letters, or take either of the word orders above and see what you come up with. Give yourself permission to have fun.

NOTEBOOK

Write these exercises in your notebook. If you do not have a notebook, get one and make it your writer's notebook. Use it only for writing in or making notes and observations for or about your writing. Buy a fancy notebook if you like them, but it may be better to buy one that is not too fancy, one that you are not afraid to use and write in. Having a lovely deluxe notebook with beautiful hand-laid paper can leave you afraid to spoil it by writing in it.

Key Idea

Your notebook is a tool – use it. One tip: buy a book with a hard cover. It is going to be with you a long, long time. You will be yanking it in and out of your bag or pocket. It needs to be able to stand up to all the rough handling it will get. Hard covers will stand up better than paper and in ten years' time, when you look back through the collection of notebooks you have gathered for hidden gems, the covers will still be on and the pages won't all fall out.

What did you come up with from these exercises? Complete nonsense? Good. You can repeat the above exercises if you wish and introduce the odd conjunction or preposition to link the words this time, but try not to do too much of that since it dilutes the challenge and makes it too logical and ordered.

Let's take the challenge to another level: a stage further.

Write

Here every word of a story or poem must begin with the same letter of the alphabet.

- Choose a letter of the alphabet (Tip: don't choose the letter z).
- Write a short piece of prose of no more than 25 words in which every word begins with that letter.

Here is a very quick attempt:

Audacious Audrey always assists angry architects; after all Australian agoraphobics ascend atriums and accumulate avalanches and austere Austrians advance absolute answers accosting angelic administrating advertisers.

Utter nonsense, again, though the 'Australian agoraphobics' and the 'angry architects' have a ring about them. Also, the idea of the 'Austrians advancing absolute answers' seems to fit the cultural stereotype of the Germanic cast of mind. It is not hard to imagine the Austrians would be clear and absolute in their answers even while they were accosting advertising administrators. We also have avalanches and architects, which seem to suggest the peaks and troughs of a landscape of contemporary buildings in a snowy setting. It is possible to see whiteness, iciness and sharp, angular lines here. And what is Audacious Audrey doing mixed up in all of it? What kind of character is she? If you do not see this, perhaps you see something else. It is quite amazing the magic in words and the pictures that odd conjunctions of words can create when seized on by eager imaginations.

If you have not done it yet, do yours; write quickly, the quicker the better.

Write

How about having another go with a timer?

- Choose a letter of the alphabet (Tip: don't choose the letter z).
- Think of a name suggested by that letter and write down a first and second name each starting with that letter, e.g. if you have chosen the letter t, you might write Terry Thomas, or Tessa Tandy. If you have chosen the letter s, the name could be Sara Sanders or Sid Smith.
- Write a short piece of prose of no more than 25 words in which every word begins with that letter.
- Set a timer for a short number of minutes, say three, and without lifting your pen from the paper or your fingers from the keyboard, write until the timer rings.

Interesting ideas can come under this sort of pressure.

Here is another one written very quickly using the letter c:

Colin Chambers, committed Catholic communist, could conveniently coddle curious custard creams continuously cursing caustic comments; casually coughing, coveting copulating Canadian canoeists, canoodling constantly, concertedly cancerous.

What a character we could have here. He loves his custard creams; he is a committed catholic communist (quite a tension there); he canoodles constantly and curses and coughs and is concertedly cancerous. In the right piece he could be a curiously colourful character.

How did you do?

HAVE FUN WITH WORDS

It is impossible to predict what you will come up with, and who knows where exercises like the one above could take you. But if they do nothing else but limber you up and give you a sense of having fun with words, then that is a good start. Play and fun are central to being creative. If something like this helps you get going, then it is a good start. You do not have to worry about starting because you have started, you are under way; suddenly you are throwing words on paper, creating images, ideas and characters; suddenly you are writing where you were not writing before and, before you know it, any block you might have had is gone.

Key Idea

Another word for creativity is FUN.

Doing exercises like these is like warming up for tai chi, dancing, running or doing some other physical activity. It is like an actor doing tongue twisters in the dressing room, limbering up lips and tongue prior to going on stage. People involved in sports warm up their bodies and their minds too, particularly if they know how to use the psychology of their sport. Warming up the mind and the imagination for writing is just as important as warming up the mind and body for movement.

The creative bubble

If you have tried to write regularly and consistently, you will also have discovered that one of the problems is having to stop. The problem with stopping is that you have to start again. You might have been in a fertile state of mind with good writing flowing from you but you have to stop through lack of time or sheer fatigue. How do you pick it up again?

The need to pick up the thread of your writing each day might take at least a few minutes, it might take even longer. Ernest Hemmingway, it is said, at the start of each day used to read the piece he was working on right the way through from the beginning to the place where he had stopped the day before and then start writing again. Other writers read the last few pages they wrote in order to get going again. This is a strategy for getting back into it, for immersing the imagination again in the world of story and characters you are creating.

Some writers, on reaching the end of a writing stint, stop midway through a paragraph or sentence thinking that that way it will be easier to pick up the thread of the story again the next day. With consistent writing, you learn the sense of having to get back into your work anew each day and of gradually getting into it as you write – that sense of warming up. And you will know that when you are warm, ideas begin to flow; you are able to create, to put down sentences that please and surprise you and move the story on or to find the character speaking in a totally unexpected way. This is creativity and it is an exciting feeling. It is what people in sport call 'being in the zone'. You may also know the feeling of frustration when you have to stop; either through time pressure or fatigue. If you know that feeling, you will know how frustrating it is that it is all so different when you do come back to it the next day or the next time. Where you were 'in the zone' before, you are outside it now and have to find that creative bubble again. How we often wish we could just pick it up again exactly where we were and carry on in that vein. If you can develop strategies to help you do that, then good. If you do not find it so easy, then perhaps playing a word game like the ones above is a strategy that might well get you loose again and back into that 'zone'. Try it next time and see.

Key Idea

'Fake it till you make it.' You need to just sit down and write something, anything. The act of writing can engage the creative mind sufficiently to get you going.

1 *Writers eavesdrop and spy, they make up stories (tell lies); they manipulate their readers.*

2 *Buy a notebook. Write in it.*

3 *Reflect on your writing practices. Think about why you write and who you write for and note it in your notebook.*

4 *Read a lot. Think about what you read. Can it help you understand what you write and who you want to write for?*

5 *Look a lot, at people and places. Listen a lot.*

6 *Read a lot. Watch movies a lot. Think about them a lot – how they work, how they are constructed, the sort of characters in them.*

7 *Write a lot.*

8 *With beginnings, the important thing is to start. Just kick the thing off and get going.*

9 *Have strategies to help you get going. If you get stuck, play writing games. Have some fun and let it loosen you up.*

10 *Whatever knock-backs you get, keep writing.*

2

Where characters come from

In this chapter you will learn:

- some simple exercises to find characters
- a few character types
- about finding characters from newspapers
- how to bring characters to life.

Where do characters come from?

Characters come from hard work on the part of the writer but they also come from fun and creative play.

Key Idea

Bringing characters into being can be creative, consuming and challenging.

Simple exercises to find characters

When we are creating a character, we can find it useful to sketch out a biography of the character: where they were born, where they went to school, what subjects they were good at, their first job, etc. One of the well-established ways of doing this is in the form of a questionnaire.

Write

Fill in the following questionnaire and see what sort of character is suggested by the answers.

CHARACTER QUESTIONNAIRE

Physical details	Background
Sex	Place of birth
Age	Marital status
Height	Residence
Weight	Occupation
Appearance	Education
Hair	Family
Scars	Parents
Defects	Kids
Illnesses	Siblings
Dress/Style	Friends
	Pets (and pets' names)

Write

What sort of character has emerged for you? Can you take this questionnaire and weave some of the answers into a short piece about the character? Imagine they are applying for a job or are being quizzed by an immigration official and write two pages based on the material in this questionnaire.

Filling in a questionnaire like the one above is a very good process to go through when seeking to find and develop characters. You can come up with all sorts of facts and background detail that you might otherwise not have thought of. Here are some more, slightly different, ways of creating characters.

Workshop: Dogs and their people

This exercise is based on an acrostic. For our purposes an acrostic is a piece of writing in which the first (or last letter) of each line spells out a word or sentence. The letters make a pattern.

Here is a single word acrostic for dog:

Daft

Obedient – not

Giant

What kind of dog is this? It is obviously a large dog; it is daft so it is full of play, perhaps it runs everywhere and does not listen to its owner. It is a Red Setter perhaps. They can be quite mad.

What kind of dog is this?

Docile

Obese

Ginormous.

This is a larger, older, slower, tired dog; perhaps more of an overweight St. Bernard? Doing this exercise is a bit of fun, but we can also make characters out of animals and they can be central characters in our stories. In fact, there are many stories that do that.

It is also said that owners look like their dogs. If this is true, you could start with the dog idea and have the beginnings of a couple of amusing human character sketches. The first example here might suggest the picture of a female owner with beautiful coppery hair (like a Red Setter) that is energetic, highly strung and quite mad. The St. Bernard with its slow gait and slobbery chops might suggest a male owner who was a bit of a couch potato, obese, television-watching and slow of movement. Developing these simple ideas could lead you from a dog to a character or two and then on to a situation.

Write

Put the tall, willowy, copper-haired, highly strung woman suggested here together with the couch potato. Write a piece where they meet through their dogs, perhaps out walking or at a dog training class. (200 words)

Case Study: Animal stories

Animals and people work well together in stories. There have been several notable books with animals as lead characters, and several popular films. The film *Turner and Hooch* had Tom Hanks as an obsessively tidy police officer forced to team up with a large, slobbery *Dogue de Bordeaux* or French Mastiff. *Marley and Me* started out as a newspaper column about the owner's relationship with a Labrador, then a book and was also made into a film. Jack London's *Call of the Wild* is a classic story of man and wolf. Clint Eastwood starred in *Every Which Way But Loose* and *Any Which Way You Can* with an orang-utan. *Tarka the Otter*, a 1927 novel by Henry Williamson, which narrates the experiences of an otter, was also made into a film. *Born Free* the 1966 feature film was based on Joy Adamson's 1960 non-fictional book *Born Free*, a story about a real-life couple who raised Elsa the lioness, an orphaned lion cub, to adulthood and released her into the wilds of Kenya. The man–animal relationship has been so well explored in fiction and film, but there is still scope for more. Who knows where such small beginnings as the exercise above might lead you? If you like and know something about animals, writing an animal story or a story with the animal as a key character could be an avenue for your writing. As is shown in the above examples, animals can make wonderful characters too.

But let's return to the idea of trying to find characters.

WHERE ELSE DO CHARACTERS COME FROM?

Characters come from observation, from research, or from learning facts about a person; they come from fragments of memory, from people you know or have known. They can come from your notebooks, from newspapers or comics, from all sorts of places and quite often from a combination of sources.

This is not meant to sound clever, but characters often come from writing. They obviously come from your dedication to the task of writing and the hard work and hours you put in and if this begins to make you feel like a coalminer, then so be it. Take on board the truth that if you did not sit at your desk – or wherever it is you work and write – if you did not put in those hours, no characters would have the opportunity to come to any of your stories. It does not mean you can't enjoy it because hard work can be highly enjoyable. But it is a dangerous lie to say that writing is easy. It is not.

Characters can also come from the requirements of the writing and the writing process itself, which can generate the need for a character. For instance, you can reach a point in a story where you realize another character is needed either to help the plot along or to give a character someone to bounce off – perhaps to provide some conflict or love interest. Or you can reach a point in a story where you realize one *less* character is needed.

HOW TO MAKE A WEAK CHARACTER STRONG

Sometimes beginning writers make the mistake of having too many characters, which diffuses them and weakens the action of the story. If you have a weak character or two in a story you are writing, see if you have too many characters. If each character by him or herself is too thin, combining a different character's desires, attitudes and characteristics with another character (or two) can make a single character stronger, more deeply layered and more complicated. Sometimes you can combine roles or purposes. By combining two or more characters into one you can make the piece stronger, give it more focus, make it less diffuse or confusing and give each character more to do, which itself can fill and round the characters off. Such characters can work on the plot in more deeply layered and complicated ways which can help the story become more layered and complex.

Write

Take a piece of your own writing and see if there are two or three characters that can be combined to make one stronger character. Try combining them in a short piece and see what happens.

Key Idea

Characters are like cocktails. As you can make one wonderful drink out of combining different ingredients, so you can make one memorable character out of combining two or three other characters.

So where do such complex cocktails of characters come from? How do we create them in the first place? Is there a process?

It is often said in writing that you should write about what you know. Who in theory do you know better than yourself? Let's do another acrostic.

Workshop: What's in a name? Part one

Take a piece of paper. Write your first name down the page, one letter beneath another, like this.

C

H

R

I

S

Now, using only one word for each letter, describe yourself honestly with simple, well-chosen adjectives. Be accurate and truthful. An initial example might be:

Calm

Helpful

Reliable

Intelligent

Sometimes

Now you do your own. Do not try to be funny or clever – no one else is going to see it but you, so you can be honest. Do it now before reading on.

What did you come up with? The first thing to look at is the overall picture.

- What sort of person do you sound like overall?
- What qualities do your words suggest?
- Are you strong and interesting?
- Are you exciting or rather boring?

Next, ask yourself

- Does any particular word stand out in your name?

Looking at the qualities suggested by the name Chris, they all sound a bit dull. Someone who is calm, helpful, reliable and intelligent is probably useful to have around but is never going to set the world alight and *certainly not in a story*, which as writers is what we want. Not only that, but he is in danger of thinking a bit too much of himself. Thank goodness therefore for the last word, 'sometimes', which undercuts the picture. If he is like this *sometimes*, what is he like the other times? If he is sometimes not calm, not helpful, not reliable, not intelligent is he a more or less interesting character? In terms of a character in life, he may be a bit difficult to live with. But if this was the picture of someone in a story, this might well be a more interesting character.

Key Idea

There are more opportunities for the character that is *not* calm, *not* helpful, *not* reliable and *not* intelligent to grow and contribute to a story than the character that is always calm, helpful, reliable and intelligent.

A few character types

Someone who is calm, helpful, reliable and intelligent all of the time could be a useful foil to someone else who has the opposite characteristics. They could be a useful secondary character: a sounding board for your hero or heroine. But if she or he were the main character in a story, you would want to test them. You would want to test their calmness, test their ability to help and be reliable; you would want to test and challenge their intelligence by putting them into situations which pit their wits against someone equally or more intelligent. You would want to see what is underneath these qualities. Look at what you wrote for yourself, the qualities you put down for your own name and ask yourself this:

If you were to be a character in a story, what sort of character would you be?

Among types of characters we can have in stories there are:

- the lead – the hero or heroine (often called the protagonist)
- a secondary character (often the best friend, the buddy, sometimes a nerd, or for comic relief)
- the lover or love interest
- the baddie (often called the antagonist).

A character that is calm, helpful, reliable and intelligent could be useful in a story but what type of character are they? Are they likely to be the lead or the lead character's buddy, the best friend and confidant? These qualities could be important in a lead character in a story but by themselves they seem to lack drive. Being helpful and reliable and intelligent are the sorts of qualities of a help mate, a secondary character, someone to assist the hero or heroine. Look again at what you listed. In terms of a character in a story ask yourself:

- Are you more the hero or heroine?
- Are you the hero or heroine's best friend? What defines this; what makes this so?
- What sorts of qualities do you think heroes and heroines need? Do you have them?
- What qualities do best friends need? Do you have them?
- Would you make a good baddie? Why?

Need is an important character quality. Your lead characters (both hero and baddie) need the sorts of qualities that are going to drive the story forward. If they lack them, then the story is likely not to move forward at the pace with which it should. This reveals an essential link between character and plot, which we will be looking at later.

Workshop: What's in a name? Part two

Let's do a little more writing about names. Think about these questions:

- Why were you named?
- What do you think of your name?
- What does it mean to you?
- Do you like your name?
- Did you ever want a different name?
- Did you ever imagine yourself with a different name?
- What was it?
- Did you have a nickname and did you like it?
- Do you have a middle name and do you like it?

Select three of these points and write for five minutes about your name. At this stage, just let the writing come; it can just be notes and fragments, it does not need to be brilliant prose. Nor do you have to spell well; you can go back over it and put all that right later. Just let it come; get something down on paper or on screen. Do it now.

When you've finished, look at what you have written and see if you have learned anything about yourself. This writing could be developed into a piece of autobiography or could form the basis for an imaginative character in a piece of fiction so keep it safe.

Now let's try the acrostics again.

Workshop: Acrostics

Make up three different acrostics of your name. You do not need to tell the truth. Be inventive. Lie. Have fun.

1 *Chris – Charming, handsome, rich, intelligent, sexy. This sounds like a personal ad but it could also be the lead in a romantic novel.*

Or:

2 *Charming, handsome, rich, irritating surgeon. This Chris could be the star of a Mills & Boon or Hallmark romance where the leading man is always so arrogant and*

annoying yet so damn attractive that the heroine can't help falling for him against her will.

But what if instead he is:

   3 *Chris – Cunning, hirsute, religious, indoctrinated, Satanist?*

Oh dear.

   4 *Chris – Challenging, hedonistic, randy, insufferable, slime ball*

   5 *Chris might be a – criminal, hirsute, religious, insufferable sod.*

Or a:

   6 *Curious, hedonistic, rebellious, irritable Scot.*

Well, they are different! How different are yours? Did you have fun? If you have not done it yet, try it now.

Once you've finished, ask yourself these questions:

- Is the character suggested by the words very different to last time?
- Is this a more interesting person than the first one or less interesting?
- Would they play a different role in a story and why?
- What role would they play?
- Would they suggest different types of situations for a story?

Let's develop it a little. What if we take our examples 1 and 3 above and put them together? What if, on the surface, Chris is a charming, handsome, rich, intelligent, sexy man but underneath a cunning, hirsute, religious, indoctrinated, Satanist? Chris might be physically clean-shaven and smooth but inside his clothes he is obviously quite hairy and, in his character, cunning and an indoctrinated Satanist. That is quite a contrast but it might lead to a much more layered character in a story. This Chris could be some sort of baddie.

Can you do something similar with two of the versions you created? Try it.

ARE CHARACTERS REAL PEOPLE?

Asking this could mean: do characters in stories come from real people or are characters in stories real? First, do characters come from real people?

Of course, some must do, and some real people believe they do and that a writer has actually written about them. One of the most famous characters in fiction, Sir John Falstaff, is thought to have been inspired by a knight by the name of John Oldcastle. Whether he was or not is of interest only to academics and scholars but from a writer's point of view, it would not be surprising. Where else are characters going to come from but real life? Dickens based some characteristics in the character of Betsy Trotwood in *David Copperfield* on a woman he met in Broadstairs, a Miss Mary Pearson, who fed him tea and cakes and ran out to chase donkeys away from her cottage. He described her cottage through the eyes of the central character, though he relocated it in the story to Dover. Dickens is not alone. Many characters in stories have a basis in life. Many also are figments of writers' imaginations, but most are probably a combination both of the observed or witnessed or known in real life and of the imagined.

Key Idea

Creating a character is more than just following someone around copying down their dialogue, or writing down their way of moving and their physical appearance. Writers put together combinations of the witnessed, observed, felt and known from separate people, drawing a little bit here, a little bit there, mixed with imagination to make a convincing whole.

In all his work, Shakespeare did not just copy someone from real life; he took many observations and mixed them up and he used imagination to make rich, deep, multi-faceted characters out of them. That is what great writers do. It is impossible to just copy someone anyway. How would you do it? Writing down an impression of someone is not copying them. A lot of portraits and pen portraits are realistic but they are not and cannot be copies of the real person. Some of Picasso's cubist portraits are not conventionally realistic. The paintings look nothing like the real people who sat for them, but the images they inspired perhaps show his emotional reaction to them rather than a desire to copy in paint what they look like in life. The real person became a springboard for his creativity.

It is a very interesting too that the converse happens. Some people not only think that characters in stories are based on real people but also that some fictional characters are real. Sherlock Homes still receives letters today from people asking him to help solve their case. The bank that currently resides at 221B Baker Street employs someone to answer them. Other people confuse actors with the characters they play, particularly in soaps and long-running television shows. It can be hard to separate the two. Because we see them every night or once a week, reading the news, or performing a part, we often think we know the people we see on television and in film, and if we ever see them in real life, we can't believe we don't actually know them.

Key Idea

No actor is the character they play. Nor is any character on a page a real person; though written well, they can seem as a real person, they can seem to come alive.

Workshop: What's in a name? Part three

Think of a name you always wished you had or make up a fantasy name. How would you be different if you were this person instead? Write a character description of the new you in 150 words. Describe yourself doing something active, such as running, cooking or fighting. Feel free to imagine; have fun. When you have done it, ask yourself these questions:

- What do you think of the character you have created?
- Is it anything like you or is it very different?
- Could you imagine this character in a story?
- What sort of story would it be?
- What would his or her role be in the story?

The acrostics on names can be a handy way of summarizing characters. They form thumbnail sketches that can suggest character flaws and even potential stories. This can be an excellent way to both sketch out and hold on to character ideas.

Write

Write three acrostics for names you like and three for names you don't like. See if you can create tension or a contradiction in two of the qualities. See that they suggest ideas about stories and genres. Perhaps the names come from a piece you are working on. If so, write them down and do the exercise with those names. The exercise may elicit new qualities or get you to think about the characters in a totally new way. They may also reaffirm the views you already have of the characters. All of this is potentially good.

Write

Write a short prose piece in which two or three of the characters you have created come into conflict over something each one of them wants badly. (200 words)

REAL AND IMAGINED WORLDS

Powerful and convincing writing can blur the boundaries between real and imagined people. When we are reading a story that we love, it is a joy to spend time with the characters in their world. We can sometimes feel that the imaginary world is more real than our real world and it can be a jolt to come out of it. The real and the imagined can blur so that we are for some moments living in a blurred space. It can be the same effect we feel when coming out of a cinema having sat through a thoroughly involving film for hours. With the all-enclosing darkness still in our heads and our eyes, with the sound, music and dialogue still in our ears, still connected and involved emotionally, often silent and not wanting to say anything but simply wanting to let the film drain away and our reactions return, we take our first few steps along the streets and slowly feel the film world dissolve and the sensations of the real world, the one we live in, return to us. Only then, after a short while, can we begin to talk about the film. Inhabiting the world of a book or story so fully can feel even more like that and can happen over an extended period of time. We love the characters in their world and can be sad to leave them. But as writers how do we create characters and worlds at all, let alone ones that are so wonderfully alive? As in all writing there is no way except through hard work and talent, but let's try two exercises that develop fictional worlds and characters from real ones.

Finding characters from newspaper stories

OBITUARIES

Obituaries are a good source for writers. They can be a good hunting ground for writers in search of characters *and* stories.

All good newspapers print obituaries each day. *The Daily Telegraph* has gathered many of their obituaries into a series of books, the *Daily Telegraph Book of Obituaries* edited by Hugh Massingberd. Each volume focuses on a different group of people such as 'Eccentrics, Rogues and Entertainers'. There are many other good sources to try too: *The Oxford Dictionary of National Biography*, *Brewer's Rogues, Villains, Eccentrics* compiled by William Donaldson (Cassell, 2002) and *Brief Lives: 150 intimate biographies of the famous by the famous*, selected by Colin Matthew (Oxford University Press, 1997).

 Write

Read some obituaries. Take one or two obituaries that you like and use them as the basis for a fictional character. Do not just copy the details of the persons' lives, but use some of the events as springboards for your own imaginings. Combine several quirks to create a richly quirky character. Write a fictional obituary of a character based on the real ones you found. (300 words)

Newspaper stories are another good source for characters.

 Write

Read some newspaper stories. Look for stories that have people in them doing something odd or unusual. They don't have to be hugely dramatic, through drama helps. They don't have to be about robbery or murder. Often the most involving drama is the drama of small events. Read several stories in several different types of newspapers and look for lively events and characters that you can use as a basis for fictional characters you can make come alive. When you have found a story that grabs you, write down the details of what happens and who it happens to in an outline. (100 words)

Bringing characters to life

Characters do need some basis in reality or some suggestion of reality about them. They also need a huge dose of the writer's imagination to bring them to life. That phrase 'to bring them to life' is an important one. How do we bring characters to life? Giving life to something inert is nothing short of miraculous. Who of us can give life to inert matter? The gods of the ancients took clay and breathed life into them. Zeus could create life. Japanese mythology believes that two divine beings went to the bridge between heaven and earth and created the islands of Japan. In Abrahamic religions, God gave life. But who of us mortals can take a handful of clay and turn it into something imbued with life?

There is a clay model in the V&A museum in London by Giovanni Bologna, also known as Giambologna. It is a model, a maquette, which is a small model of something to be made on a larger scale, of a river god. In the red clay you can see the artist's fingerprints; you can see swirls which suggest the quick movement of his hands telling us that he picked up the clay when wet and fashioned it very quickly and skilfully into what he wanted: a river god. When he put the clay down it was not the same as it had been when he first picked it up. The clay in chemical formation was no doubt identical, but what he had done with the clay had changed it forever.

The clay dried and for centuries it has held the life and the vitality of those captured moments. Giambologna's mind, and eye and hand were working at pace and in wonderful accord to make what we see before our eyes: the river god. The energy Giambologna put into the clay brought that clay to life and the life has remained there in it. It is a small miracle. Looking at that piece of mud, one can see that those artist's hands are hands that can breathe life into inert matter, like a writer can breathe life into words.

Standing close by the maquette of the river god is a huge marble statue of *Samson Slaying a Philistine*, also by Giambologna. This is one of the treasures of the V & A, one of the ten objects to see if you only have a brief time in that wonderful museum. Giambologna does the same with this work; he brings the marble to life. In terms of what it is to bring life to inert matter, Giambologna's *Samson Slaying a Philistine* is an education because various parts of the statue were at one time broken and have since been restored. For instance, the jawbone in Samson's hand, the nose of the slave, his penis and hands and feet (all the usual bits that stick out and tend to get knocked off statues over time) are not original. This was designed as part of a fountain in Florence so it has had to withstand a lot over the centuries.

If you look carefully at the statue, you can see that the magic that lay in Giambologna's hands did not lie in the hands of the craftsman who did the repairs. The marble in the original is alive; the energy of life seems to run through the surface of the marble in the same way that it does under the skin of a real living human being. It animates the muscles and sinews; it energizes the whole. The marble where Giambologna carved is energized with his artistry, his skill, and his magic. It is so powerfully lifelike, the sparkle of quartz in the marble is almost like sweat on the skin of these two men locked in mortal combat. This statue is alive in a vital way. It could come to life, though that is not the point. It is alive in its own realm as a work of art. It never will come to life in the sense of being a living, breathing thing that actually moves and ages and withers and dies. It is alive in a much greater sense, in an artistic sense. Giambologna has given the marble life. Whilst the craftsman employed to repair it has done a good job and created believable hands and feet, they are not alive in the same way. The magic stops where the repair starts; it stops at the join. There is no life in the craftsman's marble repairs. Next time you are in London, go and take a look; see for yourself the magic of a true artist and the craft of a craftsman.

The people in Rembrandt portraits can be so real, so alive, that when you are standing in front of them you imagine they could simply step out of the canvas and talk to you. There is a Rembrandt self-portrait in the Frick gallery in New York which is magnificent. The figure of Rembrandt in that assemblage of paint, canvas, wood and light is a real man. Painted centuries ago, he is as real to us as when he first painted it. In literature, Tolstoy is of the same stature of artist as Rembrandt. Both are geniuses. Each of the characters in *War and Peace* is as fully drawn, and with an economy of verbal brush strokes, as the Rembrandt portraits. Rembrandt, Giambologna and Tolstoy are masters, giants of their art, as are Mozart, Beethoven and Bach in music. The rest of us can only stand and gape at their ability with paint and words and music to make something alive and eternal. When we speak of a character 'coming alive', 'leaping off the page', we are celebrating the same marvellous thing we can see in a great artist's work. Think of the characters in Tolstoy, in Jane Austen, in Flaubert, in any of the greats. What a gift it is to give life to something. When a character comes alive for you and for your readers and audience, we all share in this same magical moment. Great artists create life. It is a gift.

It is a gift that not everyone has. Not everyone can do that; not everyone could take that clay or paint or marble and make of it a work of genius. Not everyone can make art of that calibre. The fact that not everyone can be a genius is what makes genius unique. If we could all do what Giambologna did, if we could all do what Einstein did, then discovering the theory of relativity would be just ordinary. Though it is impossible to teach anyone genius, to put magic into their hands, we can teach and others can learn what great artists do. What each individual does with that knowledge and those skills is up to them. But a lot of people can create something in art, something quite decent too.

> ## Key Idea
>
> Do not be put off if your characters do not seem to stand up to the characters in the books you like to read or the films you like to see. Keep practicing, keep trying to develop. It might take time but you can and should learn.

HOW DO WE KNOW WHEN A CHARACTER HAS COME TO LIFE?

Graham Greene is quoted in *The Plot Thickens*, by Noah Lukeman (St Martin's Griffin, 2003), saying that you know a character has come to life when the character says or does something that you had not thought about and did not expect. And after that, Greene says, you leave it to them. This is useful, pithy advice. Writers do need to let their characters speak and to listen to them and at some point the character will come to life and take over.

Characters will resist doing something 'not in character', or they will surprise you by doing or saying something unexpected. These are important moments for a writer; they are moments of life to the writer when the words come alive, when the clay has warmth and energy in it, when the pen or paint flows – and you need to accept these moments and go with them and be grateful. This is when creativity is flowing through you. You need to open yourself to it and be the vessel through which it comes.

When they do take on a power and energy of their own, when they do come to life, the proper response to a character is one of gratitude and respect. Let them come, let them speak, let them act, let them live. Give yourself over to that power and welcome it. And let the writing serve, let it be responsive to the character's dreams, desires and decisions, and do not impose upon the character what does not fit and what does not suit. The character will develop integrity and a core beyond which any attempts to force it will fail. As a writer you need to be responsive to the character. Your writing is to help them live and breathe and act and do. Writing that stands in the way of that, which intrudes itself between the reader and the character, which draws attention to itself, is not doing its proper job.

10 TIPS FOR SUCCESS

1 *Creating characters comes from hard work and the process of writing.*

2 *Combining one or two weak characters can be a good way of creating one strong, deep character with layers.*

3 *Do not confuse characters in stories with real people. Characters in stories can be more real than real people.*

4 *Naming a character is a hugely important decision. A character can take form around the right name.*

5 *Qualities a character possesses can be suggested by the name they have.*

6 *A character can love or hate their name and this can lead them into situations that writers can exploit.*

7 *Characters with only good qualities are not always going to be the best characters in a story. Characters need a mix of good and bad qualities to make them come alive and be interesting to readers.*

8 *Starting with a character type does not mean you have to finish with a stereotype. It can be useful to start out with a two-dimensional character type and fill it out.*

9 *The hero, villain and lover can be a skeletal framework on which to build the flesh of a truly rounded and memorable character.*

10 *Characters with an inner tension, or who feel a conflict between two desires or qualities, will bring this tension to a story and make it potentially more interesting than characters with no inner tension or conflict.*

3

Strategies for improving your writing

In this chapter you will learn:

- about working with outlines
- how to put up scaffolding to build a piece of writing
- about polishing a piece of writing
- how to make your writing concrete.

Working with outlines

In the previous chapter we discussed the fact that fictional characters can be based on real people. We also suggested newspapers as a good source of character. Here is an example of an outline written from an original newspaper story.

> *Harry Sanders, 38 lives in a flat in East London with his 29-year-old Scottish girlfriend Carol Edwards. He is desperately looking for work, having given up a lucrative job in the city to nurse Carol who is suffering from MS. But work is not easy to find for someone with a coke habit, which he acquired through various high-flying friends in the city who have now deserted him.*

This example has two characters, both of them with problems and a real need. There is the chance that we can develop both characters and a story from this. You try.

Write

Find a piece in a newspaper and write it as an outline for a piece of fiction.

An important point to note here is that an outline, such as the one above, is not the finished story. It is another tool on the way to a story. To develop this point further, let's look in detail at the paragraph above. Look back at it again and read it over.

What did the paragraph read like to you? It probably reads like an introduction, a synopsis of the 'story so far', after which we expect the story to start. It reads like background, the sort of notes we would write for ourselves in order to get to grips with the characters and their backgrounds. It is in fact a summary, perhaps part of an outline for a story we are going to write. It is not the story itself, but something leading up to the story. In truth, none of this should appear in the finished piece, *in this form*.

The opening sentence of the paragraph sounds like it has actually come from a newspaper; it is the sort of sentence where the reporter packs in as much information as he or she can. 'Harry Sanders, 38 and his 29-year-old Scottish girlfriend Carol Edwards.' The last sentence suffers from the same thing. The writing is reportage. And this is actually what is wrong with it in this context. We are being told about the two characters and their situation; we are not being taken *into* their situation and their world and being given the chance to share it with them. This is absolutely fine for an outline or a reminder, some notes we will have written for ourselves, but the story itself demands a different approach. Notes like these are good to get going as shorthand. The problem comes when they somehow get left in pieces of writing, when we forget to take them out.

Key Idea

It can be a useful to write an outline, but an outline is not a story.

How to put up scaffolding to build a piece of writing

Often in the writing of the piece we need to put markers down. Sometimes these are notes for ourselves, like marking out a plot of land for a building.

Building is a good metaphor for writing. Builders work from detailed architects' drawings or blueprints. They have a plan. The building is conceived in the mind of an architect, but when it comes to the actual building process, builders need to lay foundations and mark out the ground to show where the walls and doors are going to go and so on. After this, to start building upwards they need to put up scaffolding. To build our writing, we too need scaffolding; we need a framework. We need something down on paper that we can build on. An outline is the blueprint on which we can build.

How detailed we need our plans to be will depend on the sort of writer we are and perhaps the sort of piece we are writing. But we always put some scaffolding up whether we are conscious of it or not. We put up scaffolding because with it we can write; we can begin to realize the piece of work from a concept in our minds to a reality that others can share and inhabit. Without the scaffolding, we would not be able to build.

Our scaffolding could be an outline draft. It will also be made up of, for instance, the research we have done, the notes we have made about characters and places. The character questionnaire included in the previous chapter would also allow you to come up with the sorts of details that are necessary to know as a writer, but *that may well have no place in the story*. Knowing facts like the ones you filled in on the questionnaire can help you to know the characters in your mind, and when you are writing you can also find it useful to put some of these details into the story as part of the process of writing the character, of creating them. You might feed them into a piece of description, into a piece of back story about their school life, or into a piece of dialogue, only to become aware later that you need to cut them out because they are unnecessary for the finished piece. You can discover, on revision, that these are supports and that the piece is stronger without them. But you put them in because they are a way of getting going, a way of building, a way of supporting what you are writing. They are the scaffolding poles and planks of wood on which you can build until you find the true form of words you want to use. You might also put them in because you can't think of anything better yet. They are a kind of blank that you use to fill a gap for now and which allows you to go on with the writing. You know you will come back and put the real bit in later, though problems can arise if you forget. This idea of scaffolding is familiar to creative artists working across different fields: novelists, playwrights, screenwriters and songwriters.

Case Study: Yesterday

When Paul McCartney was composing the song 'Yesterday' he got the melody very quickly but could not find a title or the lyrics. He and John Lennon called the song 'Scrambled Eggs'. They needed to work on it so they had a working opening verse which went 'Scrambled Eggs/Oh, my baby how I love your legs.'

This is clearly very different to the finished version but the temporary structure of these lyrics, the scaffolding, allowed them to progress. Instead of staying where they were and being stuck they put anything down so as to keep the idea growing. This is scaffolding.

Let's look at scaffolding in some other pieces of writing and look at the following technique.

Polishing a piece of writing

Here is another example. This writer, a student, was asked to write a piece, five sentences long, using all of the five senses.

The girl's unseeing eyes followed the tap-tap of her cane. Her nose quivered as she passed a bakery. Her hand touched the window pane. Her lips tasted the imagined pastry.

It is a good enough start. It is actually four sentences but the five senses are there, including sound in the 'tap-tap of her cane'. It also has the feel of a poem to it. You might think that it is such a small piece of writing that there could not be anything redundant, but all writing can be condensed and more focused. So, let's have a look to see if there is anything in it like scaffolding that we could look at and improve. The first sentence, 'The girl's unseeing eyes followed the tap-tap of her cane' is economical. It gives us a good story set up. We are introduced to a character, a girl, she has a predicament, 'unseeing' tells us she is blind and she is in a situation, i.e. walking along the street with her cane. We have a blind girl walking along a street with her cane. But let's ask some questions here.

First, we could ask if we need 'unseeing?' Would not the tap-tap of her cane do the job as well, as in 'The girl followed the tap-tap of her cane?' You might ask 'What if she were lame? Could she not be using a stick because she has a limp?' This is something the rest of the piece could clarify. But is not the change we have made better because now the image of the girl following the tap-tap of the cane suggests blindness without saying it? We can see the cane stretching out in front of her, probing, while the rest of her follows and maybe we can even hear the cane striking against the pavement better. So, removing the scaffolding word 'unseeing', put in by the writer to ensure we understood the point of the blindness, allows a stronger image to emerge. It is quite common in writing for the writer to spoil a good image by not trusting it, by adding explanation to shore it up. Writers need to trust their images.

Key Idea

Don't explain: trust the image.

The next sentence in the piece, as stories should, introduces a development and a complication, 'her nose quivered as she passed a bakery'. This takes the piece on and introduces the idea of hunger. Could we improve this at all? Let's look at what the student has written: 'Her nose quivered as she passed a bakery.' Why is her nose quivering? It is quivering because it smells something. What does it smell? Her nose smells baking. The trouble with the phrase 'as she passed a bakery' is that it could suggest that she knows the bakery is there without smell at all. Perhaps she walks this way often and knows the bakery is on this street, in which case she does not need her nose to tell her there is a bakery nearby. Her nose tells her something is baking but not that there is a bakery nearby. What is missing here is that moment when, through the smell, she realizes there is a bakery close by. What if we cut out the little phrase 'as she passed' so that the sentence read: 'Her nose quivered – a bakery?' Now she is no longer passing a bakery that she knows is there and it makes the bakery's nearness more uncertain. The bakery could be a distance away, nor does she know for certain that it is a bakery. Because we get a suggestion of her sense of smell working to give her information and of her processing that information, the picture is immediately more active and alive and this actually increases the sense of her blindness. We can see her thinking and, as readers, we can share in it. The bakery is a pleasant surprise, both for the character and for us, and we become much more engaged readers.

What about the rest of the piece? 'Her hand touched the window pane. Her lips tasted the imagined pastry.' The first part brings the sense of touch into play and at the end we have the sense of taste where she imagines the pastry. Can we do anything to improve this? The first part has a solid sense of touch in it. It is an action of reaching out and touching, which grounds the piece, making it concrete. Let's focus instead on the last part 'Her lips tasted the imagined pastry.' Is there anything like scaffolding here that we could remove? Again, let's look precisely at what we have written.

 ## Key Idea

Always look precisely at what you have written. If you are having a problem with a section of writing, the problem can only lie in what you have written, in the words you have put down and your intention – what you wanted to say in those words. Perhaps they are inadequate and fail to get across what you wanted, or maybe they are plain dull and need stripping out and starting again. Study them carefully, look at each word to see where the problem lies and what cutting and replacing may be required. Maybe they do something other than what you wanted, but better. In that case, accept it and give thanks.

'Her lips tasted the imagined pastry.' Why the 'imagined' pastry? Because the author wants to tell us that the girl is outside the shop and cannot see the pastry, so has to imagine it. Also, she has not got her hands on the real pastry yet. What the writer is doing here is underlining the fact that the girl is blind. But we already know this. Why does the writer feel the need to tell us this again, given that the writer has already established the girl's blindness at the start of the piece? Maybe the writer is afraid that we will not get the point that the girl is blind, that she cannot actually see the pastry and so has to imagine it. It is recapping at the end what the writer has told us at the beginning, i.e. that this is a story about a blind girl. But is not such fear mistaken? What if we take out the word 'imagined' and also revise the end slightly so that the piece now reads as follows?

The girl followed the tap-tap of her cane. Her nose quivered – a bakery. Her hand touched the window pane, lips tasting pastry.

There is still one point here: lips don't taste, the tongue does, so we had better change lips to tongue. Suddenly it is a much tauter piece and is more alive. Why? Because there is action and activity where there was none before and we share the girl's sense and experience. Not only does the smell of baking reach her (and us) and actively get her thinking, but also once she thinks 'a bakery', we can actually see her stretch out her hand and search for the window pane. We see her outside the shop and our taste buds almost taste with hers the pastry she can smell. She does not really taste it, it *is* imagined, and because it is now much more strongly imagined by her, we imagine tasting it too. The piece is much stronger and alive because the writer removed the scaffolding.

Key Idea

Scaffolding is all of the props and supports put in to help us negotiate the actual writing of the piece.

Scaffolding comes when we tell readers too much. We put in the type of writing analysed above to help us when we are working on the piece. We put markers down. Such markers can also sometimes be writing on the way to find what it is we are writing. That is to say, we are uncertain of a piece, in some ways uncertain what exactly we are doing; we need to write to allow the idea to form. But once we have found that idea, once it has formed, we need to revise and focus; the scaffolding must come down. The piece we have edited is now also more intelligent. It is written for a more intelligent reader who can enter into the story and think. Never think that just by adding more to a piece that we can improve it.

Key Idea

If you have a problem with a section of writing, never think you can just write a bit more, adding more words to explain the bit that is not working. Your first move should always be to try and put the problem area right. Focus on that; look at what exactly you are saying and try to decide why it is not working. Be prepared to take whole sections out and start again rather than just adding more words. Adding more words is just shoring up something that is inadequate in the first place.

Scaffolding also comes from fear. Our writing is built, added to, constructed, and we can be afraid the edifice we have erected will not be strong enough to stay up without the scaffolding we have put in place to help the process. But we must trust ourselves and above all we must trust our readers. Even in a world that appears to be dumbing down everything around us, the more writing of intelligence that gets produced, the more intelligent readers will demand it – and that can only be good for writing and publishing. We must trust our readers.

Key Idea

Write for intelligent readers and trust them.

Write

Now we have edited and focused this piece, we have the beginnings of a piece with a strongly suggested central character. There are many directions in which this piece with the blind girl could go. Maybe she meets someone at the shop? Maybe she has an accident. Maybe she helps someone. Take this character on into a story and see what happens to her. (500 words)

Workshop

To further practise polishing a piece of writing, let's consider another piece. These are the first few notes in a writer's notebook of an observed moment. It is hardly an incident.

On coming outside, talking fast a young man sneezed twice, loud explosions, then walked on. Sun lit up the beautiful droplet drift. I moved on, fast.

This is a writer noting something that interests him and writing it down, something that he might later use. But what is it that has interested him? A young man sneezing? Why? Your task is to do what we did before and look precisely at what has been written.

There is a lot of movement in the notes. A young man comes out of a building; he is talking fast and presumably moving fast. He sneezes twice. They are loud 'explosions' so he presumably does not cover his nose and then he carries on walking, still fast. The writer speedily notes it down while it is fresh. He notes the movement, the sound, the sneezes and the drift of droplets caught in sunlight and there is humour at the end where the writer scuttles out of the way of the drifting droplets so that he does not catch a cold. Why did this moment interest him? He is a writer. But what do these notes contain and what is there in this jotting that has potential for later development? Can we find a character here?

Compare these two pieces of writing:

1 On coming outside, talking fast a young man sneezed twice, loud explosions, then walked on. Sun lit up the beautiful droplet drift. I moved on, fast.

2 Leaving class talking fast, a young student sneezes twice – loud explosions. Clear sunlight shows the golden droplet-drift shoot from his nose.

What is the difference between these two pieces of writing? Version one has changed into version two through the same process of polishing carried out on the piece about the blind girl above but what has changed? Make a list of the changes and try and see why the writer has developed the piece of writing in this way.

There is a detailed account of the polishing the writer went through to get to this stage in the appendix. Look at the two versions; work out what has been changed and why and then check the appendix out to see the steps that were taken and whether you agree with them.

Making your writing concrete – avoid empty words

There is an empty word in the first version of the notes about the sneeze. It is a marker word which is not really contributing the piece; it is just filling up a space and is a definite bit of scaffolding. What is the empty word? Read the first version again.

> *On coming outside, talking fast a young man sneezed twice, loud explosions, then walked on. Sun lit up the beautiful droplet drift. I moved on, fast.*

The word is 'beautiful'. What kind of word is the word beautiful? It is a noun; more specifically, it is what is called an abstract noun. The words 'table', 'apple' and 'finger' are concrete nouns; we can apprehend them with our senses and we can touch and smell and see them. An abstract noun is something we cannot touch and smell and see. Examples of abstract nouns are 'poverty', 'happiness', 'eternity' and 'beauty'. There is obviously a place for all of these words and for abstract nouns like 'beautiful' or they would not exist in our language, but the problem with the abstract word 'beautiful' in a piece of creative writing is that it *is* abstract – it is empty until we fill it with content. We can say someone is beautiful but does that help us see why? Do we know what they look like? No we do not. Does the word beautiful convey what makes someone beautiful? No, it does not. In this context it is an empty word and not needed. That is why the writer changed the word 'beautiful' to 'golden' in the final draft. He was trying to help us see.

Key Idea

When people are asked to express their feelings on the radio or television about something that has occurred to them they often take refuge in empty words. They will say it was 'beautiful', 'fantastic' or it was 'incredible' or 'amazing' – none of which conveys to anyone what the experience was like. In truth, they cannot tell us what it was like because the experience was so amazing, or fantastic, or incredible that it is beyond their ability to describe it, probably beyond most people's ability to describe. But we expect writers to be able to describe such experiences to us. That is their job. We expect a writer to write the experience in such a way that we can experience it too. That is what such good writing is about.

Workshop: From a writer's notebook

Read the following notes from a writer's notebook of a small interaction between a girl, a dog and a mother.

Her Mum had tied the yapping dog up outside the cafe. The girl told the dog to stop barking and then she came into the cafe. When the dog yapped again the girl screwed her face up and stomped out again. She pointed a finger at the dog and made a stern face, the way she'd seen her Mum do many times before to her. Looking at her, the dog stopped yapping. Satisfied the girl went back in. The dog yapped again.

- *Girl: Pink mittens, tights in coloured bands like liquorice allsorts, pink, brown, white and cream like a Neapolitan ice cream. A pink and brown waterproof top and pink mittens, her blonde hair pulled back from her face.*

- *Dog: Spiky biscuit-coloured hair in his eyes, tongue hanging out. Mud in small black socks up his short furry legs and hanging from the undersides of his thick, ragged fur. Bouncing on his leash and jumping up each time someone new came near to the post to which he was tied.*

- *The girl had a pink T-shirt on with a steaming mug of hot drink in a red cup on the front.*

- *She had a small, mobile face that could scowl, look puzzled, thoughtful and interested, one after another. Black sandals with her striped stockings peeking through.*
- *'You're making him bark by going in and out,' said her Mum.*

Your task is to work these notes up into a short prose piece. Don't write masses. Just try to stay with the scene that *you* can find in the notes. Change the sentences around, put them in a different order, add to them, cut bits about, but try to stay faithful to the original vision, to what comes over in the notes and what interested the writer. 'Worry' over it the way we have just done in the example. There is no right or wrong way to do this – see what you come up with – but there is a version in the appendix for you to look at after you have done yours. Just go through the process, and compare yours later if you wish. Keep it short and tight. (300 words)

 ## Key Idea

When you have finished a piece, a story, opened the building and invited all the dignitaries in for the grand opening, it does not make a good impression to leave the scaffolding up. Scaffolding is a means, a tool; it helps us build but then has to be taken down. The problem can be that sometimes as writers we get so used to the scaffolding that we become blind to it; we have used it as a crutch and can't envisage the work without it, or we are so used to it that we don't see it anymore.

A FINAL WORD ON SCAFFOLDING

Doing the exercise above, you will not have used everything in the notes – you will have left some parts out and made up others and this is always the same with pieces of writing, this is how we work. That bit of information about a character's background – that helpful scene explaining the character's key motive, explaining why he or she has committed adultery or murdered someone, the explanation that someone is blind or that a scene is beautiful – will not be necessary. It may, in fact, mar the story. However when it is pointed out to us and we take down the scaffolding of explanation, when we cut the pieces of explanation, introduction and support, the piece we have created can be seen by itself and for itself and can suddenly come alive. Shorn of scaffolding, we can see the building as it stands, and it can be beautiful, because we can see what makes it so.

The reason this happens is that once we cut away phrases like the ones in the first example that tell the reader a little about our characters and their situation, our ears prick up and the imagination is engaged. When we as writers spot a piece of scaffolding that is too general or abstract and has no content, then once we provide the content, our readers can engage more deeply. If a reader is not told about who this or that person is, or what this or that situation or setting is, the reader's mind itself has to think and make judgements and is therefore more active. A good writer will feed the imagination; they will give the imagination just enough clues to feed on. The imagination likes to be active and not fed drugged food.

Key Idea

It is one thing to spot a weakness or a problem in a piece of writing, but quite another to put it right. A critic can spot a weakness in a piece of writing; he can never put it right. That is the writer's job.

A FURTHER FINAL WORD ON SCAFFOLDING

Do we always take scaffolding down? Just as when composing the song 'Yesterday' Lennon and McCartney used scaffolding to keep the project going forward, a similar thing happened with a Carpenters song called 'Yesterday Once More'. The chorus of this song goes 'Every sha-la-la-la / Every wo-wo-wo / Still shines / Every shing-a-ling-a-ling / That they're starting to sing / So fine.' These nonsense words are bits of scaffolding. The composers could not think of the right lyrics, so they just sang this nonsense to allow the song to grow and be worked on. In the end they decided that they liked the nonsense lyrics and that they worked, so they stayed in – and if you like the Carpenters' song, they work. This is a case of the scaffolding being incorporated into the finished building. This happens too in contemporary art, architecture, music and writing.

Towards the end of *Money*, by Martin Amis, the author writes himself into the story and engages in a dialogue with the main character, trying to warn him about the likely end of his behaviour and being criticized by the character who talks back to him. Not only are the mechanics of the piece shown here, but the architect of the piece – the man who put up all the scaffolding – walks into the picture to tell us it is all a picture. This is rather like making the scaffolding feature as part of the final work. This particular intrusion also raises larger questions about the nature of the novel and what a work of art is – a discussion which is outside the scope of this book. But so far as scaffolding goes, suffice it to say that as long as it works and creates something creative, engaging and revealing for the reader, and you, the writer, sanction it, then leaving scaffolding as part of the design is ok. Accidentally leaving a bit of scaffolding up is not what should happen.

10 TIPS FOR SUCCESS

1 *Put up scaffolding to help you write. Sometimes you need to put in something just for the sake of being able to move on. Remember to come back later and revise.*

2 *Get to love revision. Think of it as a chance to look again, as a 're-vision' of the piece, a chance to get to the freshness of the first inspiration.*

3 *Polish your writing. Test every word to see if it is doing the job you want it to do.*

4 *Love the process of writing, changing and cutting.*

5 *Look for empty words and phrases, words that can be improved and do more work.*

6 *Trust the image.*

7 *Write for intelligent readers, readers you trust.*

8 *Make notes in your notebook of the little and big observations and ideas that interest you. Worry the notes over later to see what they might yield.*

9 *We might not always take scaffolding down but we must never leave scaffolding up by accident.*

10 *Give abstract words concrete content.*

4

Inside out or outside in

In this chapter you will learn:

- how to create characters from inside out and outside in
- how to make characters from simple, everyday items of clothing
- about flat and round characters.

Creating characters from inside out or outside in

There are at least two key ways to create characters: from outside in or from inside out. These are the same two ways that many actors use to work on their parts.

 ## Key Idea

Writers can learn a lot from actors. If you are writing scripts, it is crucial that you work with actors or get some experience of how an actor will work on a script, what they look for in a part, the insights they have about character drive and construction. Actors really pick into a script and ask questions about every word and every motive and move a character makes. This process can be painful and difficult but invaluable for a writer.

Actors who say something like 'once I get the walk right, I can get the part' are interesting. Is this working from outside in or from inside out? Are they trying to get what the walk *looks* like from outside or what it *feels* like from within? The approaches are different. Someone walking naturally, just because they are walking, will walk differently from someone walking because they think someone else is watching them. Imagine Juliet walking into a room with Romeo in it. Knowing Romeo's eyes are upon her, she will walk differently to the way she walks in front of her family or about her rooms alone or when she is talking with her nurse or the friar. She is going to be so excited. She might take quicker, shorter steps. Her heart rate will increase and her breathing will change. Presumably a model up on the catwalk walks differently when home alone. One can only hope so!

An actor who needs the walk, the costume, the make-up and clothing, who needs to get the accent right to feel the part, is in a way impersonating the character in the manner of American actors Meryl Streep (*Out of Africa* and *The Devil Wears Prada*), Dustin Hoffman (*Midnight Cowboy*, *Marathon Man*, and *Tootsie*), Welsh stage and film actor Michael Sheen, who played Tony Blair in *The Deal*, *The Queen* and *The Special Relationship*, David Frost on stage and film in *Frost/Nixon*, and Brian Clough in *The Damned United*. They are all probably working from outside in, though these outside factors will impinge and work on and affect the inner life. These actors are working from the external appearance, the mannerisms, the voice, to find the character within.

An actor who works on the character's desires, wants and needs is trying to find ways to portray them outwardly from within. *These* characters will perform the actions they do and speak the words they speak because of the needs and desires they have. The desires, wants and needs bring into being the character and their actions, not the costume, accents or appearance. This would be the approach of arguably the best British stage and screen actor of the middle and late twentieth century, Laurence Olivier, and arguably the best American film actor of his time, Robert Duvall. These two actors change what they look like only a little using costume and other external devices – the real change comes from within. Physically, Robert Duvall looks from the outside much the same from part to part, but inside from part to part the characters he plays are truly different people, and this somehow changes the sense of him physically. We believe in the character he is portraying. His portrayal of mass murderer Adolf Eichmann in *The Man Who Captured Eichmann* was a wonderful piece of acting that had power to elicit surprising sympathy from the audience. From out of Duvall's eyes there was another, different human being looking at us. Duvall's performance justly got him nominated for an Emmy award. His Eichmann was certainly a rounded, three-dimensional figure and Duvall was able to show that he had a point of view. This man, a villain in so many people's eyes, was the hero in his own story.

Key Idea

Villains are heroes in their own stories.

This is a point well worth underlining. It will be important for your writing that you realize villains really are heroes in their own stories. In fact, *everyone is a hero in their own story*. Sometimes what is wrong with the heroes (the protagonists) in stories is that the villain (the antagonist) is not strong enough. Whereas a good, strong, credible villain will bring the best out in the hero, a weak villain gives a hero nothing to do. To overcome a strong villain, the hero will need to draw on greater reserves of character, strength and energy. This brings a better energy to the whole story and adds to the dynamic tension between the goody and the baddy.

One of the crucial ways to give your antagonist strength is to ensure they have a point of view. The other characters in the story may think the villain's outlook on life is not right; you may think the villain is not right, but what you think does not matter. It is what your character thinks that matters. The villain needs to believe what they are doing in the story; the villain needs to have their own justifiable point of view, justifiable by their own logic, and quite possibly twisted logic, but justifiable to them. As a writer your job is not to agree with your villain but to make sure their character expresses what they believe. You are not there to censure or to judge your characters but to help them live. The more you can get inside your characters, villains and heroes, the more chance you have of creating strong, real, credible people for your stories. Whether creating 'goodies' or 'baddies', heroes or villains, you can come to them either way, from inside out, or from outside in. Both ways work.

Though the characters we write, like real people, are made up of both what is outside and what is inside, it can be quite difficult to separate the inner and the outer, for they obviously interact with each other in an essential way. But for the sake of developing an argument here, it can be useful to look at character creation from both approaches.

In brief, characters are made up of what we apprehend from *outside*, what they look like physically: the colour of their eyes, skin and hair, their height, weight, their accent and the sound of their voice; all those pieces of physical information (except about voice) that we all would put down on a passport form. Characters are also characterized by the clothes and jewellery or make-up they wear, if they wear any at all. And characters are also made up of what is *inside*, what we don't see: their desires, needs, wants, hopes and emotions, their entire inner life. As writers you can start to create characters either way, from wants and needs outwards, or from outward appearance inwards.

We will start here from outside in.

Creating characters from outside in

Working from outside in, you can use one of the main components of character creation: description. As we have just said above, you can describe the colour of a character's hair, eyes, or skin, or anything about them. You can tell us they have a squint, that they limp, or that they chain smoke. You can also start by describing what they are wearing.

Key Idea

In terms of the writing process and in terms of finding a character, discovering as many physical attributes about them as we can, plus the clothing they wear, can be a helpful way into them. How much of this you leave in the finished book or story will be up to you, and will depend, like the rest of the writing, on what works in that particular instance. This early research may well end up in the bin, but you need to start somewhere and this is a good place to do that.

UNIFORMS

In general, our clothing is not accidental. In life, if we have a choice, we choose to wear what we like or what suits us. Often in different circumstances we also have to wear what we did not choose or would not have chosen. Prisoners, for instance, are not given a choice of what to wear; the uniform they are given and the lack of choice is part of what defines them as prisoners. Their street clothes are taken away and they are given a prison uniform to make them identical and easy to spot as well as to punish them. When we are working, the job we do may dictate a uniform, from a simple business suit to a soldier or a nurse's uniform, or the ermine of a member of the House of Lords. They all have requirements and those requirements of dress can define the role and us within that role. This is all very useful for a writer. Inhabiting a uniform can also define an entire character for an actor.

Case Study: Scent of a Woman

In *Scent of a Woman* Al Pacino's character, the blind, drunken and angry retired army ranger, Lieutenant Colonel Frank Slade, puts his uniform on with dignity and with care when he has finally decided to take his own life. The uniform has been his life. He identifies with the uniform and needs to complete this final act of suicide in it. He dresses slowly and meticulously, fully conscious and aware of what he is going to do. He does so with a finality of decision that makes the donning of the uniform a powerful symbol of his life and his need for what the army gave him, for what he has lost and will regain in death. It is a powerful moment in a part for which the actor received an Academy Award for best actor.

The *screenplay* was an adaptation and though it did not win the Academy Award, it is award-worthy writing too. The character of Lt. Col. Frank Slade is a man who needs to be in uniform. The outside shell of the uniform is essential to his character but is also very strongly part of what is going on inside him and is a good example of the connection between outer and inner: of the outer leading us into the inner core of the character. He could only complete the task of the inner character by wearing the outer uniform.

Write

Write a short piece of prose in which a character puts on a uniform. Start with the character in ordinary clothes in an ordinary, everyday world. He or she puts on the uniform and as they do so they assume a different character, the character dictated by the uniform. The character should have changed by the end of the piece so that he or she is a different person. Possible uniforms are a police or service uniform, a surgeon, a nurse or matron, the rig-out of a judge, a traffic warden or an undertaker. (300 words)

Example: creating a character from outside in

Here is another simple exercise that starts outside with an item of clothing. It starts with observation.

Imagine you are in an airport departure lounge, waiting for your flight to be called. Your eyes are down, you are reading or you are tired and all you can see above your book is a pair of shoes. Yes, someone is in the shoes but all you can see are the shoes. You cannot see the owner of the feet in the shoes yet because you have not looked up. Don't look up yet, just look at the shoes that have caught your eye. Why? There must be something about them to catch your eye. They can't just be like every other pair of shoes in the world. Nor do they have to be outlandish pink high-heels or huge purple boots to catch your interest. They could be quite ordinary but what is it that catches your eye? Let's focus the question: is it the shoes or is it something attached to the shoes? Perhaps a ribbon is hanging from them or a large piece of chewing gum or something else is stuck to the soles.

Let's assume it is the shoes that catch your interest. First of all what kind of shoes are they? There are so many different kinds of shoes in the world from sandals to brogues but let's say, for example, that you see a pair of trainers. Brand new trainers? They could be brand new; that might catch our interest. But let's say that these are once-white trainers with red laces and soiled toes. That is quite simple and not over dramatic. It is quite ordinary in fact. Trainers that start out white will easily end up grubby with toes slightly soiled with a little bit of wear. Now, what else can you see? You can see the size and condition of the shoes, so what size are they? Are they big, or are they small? Are they on the feet of a giant or a child? Don't look up; pretend you can't see the person. Let's say the shoes are not incredibly tiny, nor extra large. They are average. (Average is not a favourite word for a writer, it will normally spell death by boredom, but starting with average is okay; it depends what you do with it.)

Let's say they are big enough to be an average man's shoes. Next, what condition are the shoes in? Apart from being soiled, how do they look? Any splits, cracks, other signs of wear? Do they look like they are someone's favourite shoes and have been nearly worn into the ground? Let's say that apart from having dirty toe-caps they are not in bad shape. They are not brand new but not that old either. (Be careful, we are dangerously close to that middle of the road average thing again.) But let's say that these shoes are not split or otherwise worn and old, they are in good shape, they are just a bit grubby. They are in fact quite ordinary; there is nothing truly special about them.

So, now, before you raise your eyes, think – what would you expect to go with these shoes? What kind of feet are in these shoes? Are they young feet, old, tired, swollen, wrinkled? You could write several paragraphs about the feet to help you begin to imagine the character. What sort of legs in what kind of apparel would you expect to see? The real question we are asking here is: what expectations do these shoes raise and how are we, as writers, going to answer them?

Key Idea

Our writing sets up expectations in the reader. We need to play along to a certain extent with these expectations as we develop the writing in order to use them to the reader's advantage later, to increase their enjoyment.

We have a bit of focus now: we are looking at a pair of once-white men's trainers with red laces and soiled toes. Now there could be a man or a woman's feet in these trainers. Even if the shoes are man-sized they could be being worn by a woman with big feet. But let's stay with the obvious for the moment. In that case, it is reasonable for us to say that we would expect to see a man in man's shoes. Above the trainers it would also not be a surprise to see a pair of jeans, turned up three inches at the bottom with dirty cuffs. And let's say that that is what we do see. Now, going higher, let's say that you see that the jeans are suitably grubby and distressed. Higher still, the blue sweat-shirt with 'UCLA' on it in yellow/gold lettering seems to belong, as does the young man in his early 20s in the jeans and trainers and T-shirt who is listening to his iPod. So far, so expected. Sitting in an airport lunge you could easily make observations about the person opposite you and with your writer's notebook begin to write about him. The notes might for instance be like this: 'young man – Heathrow airport London waiting for the 9.55 a.m. flight to Los Angeles, California. Young student going back to University. (UCLA stands for University of California Los Angeles.)' And so on.

And if you seriously want to write, this is exactly what you should be doing. You should be noticing what is around you and putting down notes about it, partially because you never know when such notes are going to be useful and when you are going to use them, but also because you are keeping yourself in shape as a writer. You are doing daily exercises of observation and writing and as a writer you need to exercise as much as any more obviously physical activity, such as being a musician or athlete. You can exercise standing in a line at the supermarket checkout, in the waiting room of a doctor's surgery or in the departure lounge of an airport; you need to be looking, thinking, noting and writing down. And you must write it down; if you don't you will forget it. You may think you won't forget, but you will.

 ## Key Idea

Writing takes muscles, both mental and physical; daily exercises of these muscles will keep you in shape. Wherever you are, standing in a line at the supermarket checkout or in the departure lounge of an airport, you need to be looking, thinking noting and writing observations down: thoughts, ideas, snatches of dialogue and description. Get into the habit of observing people.

ORDINARY PEOPLE

So far we are going mostly with the ordinary. But remember, we don't have to stick with what we see. We can use that but we also have imaginations, which can help us to add to the pictures we develop. Let's see what we can do with the picture we have been developing of the young man. Let's now say 'he drives an expensive (or battered) open-topped car and lives in student accommodation or with his girlfriend in downtown LA or his father and mother in Beverley Hills.' We can *see* the trainers, jeans and T-shirt, but not the car he drives or where he lives. We have made that bit up. Yet even so, it is so far all of a piece. We can imagine the bit about the car and where he lives to be true and think of other elements that seem to go with the picture, but trying to make all the bits fit could in itself be a mistake. Or, if not a mistake, not the only route we could go. If we make it all fit, there is nothing unexpected in it. If we were to begin now to flesh it out with some other detail, real or imagined, about his background, networks of friends and so on, we could keep developing a predictable portrait. But what other approach could we take? We could make more up and not be limited by what might or might not be expected.

Key Idea

As writers, we pretend and invent and twist the facts. We use what we see and hear and sense to make up stories. *We lie.*

Or, let's put it another way and say that we take what seems like reality and turn it into another reality on the written page. Writers have freedom: a license to imagine and to create. Use it.

We have already alluded to this different approach. If we had made the feet in the shoes belong to a woman, we could have developed a different sort of character. Though the man's shoes might reasonably have been expected to be worn by a man, we could have confounded expectations by having them worn by a woman. We would still then have had to go on and further characterize the woman to fill her out and make her interesting but the principle of setting up one expectation and confounding it with something else makes the character less 'average' and more engaging for the reader.

Key Idea

We may have to start with ordinary, the everyday, the observed, but we do not have to stay there. We have to find ways to make the characters in our stories stand out in a crowd; why else would we follow them through the hell and high water of a story?

TYPES AND STEREOTYPES

How do we develop less ordinary characters? First of all, let us make clear that some characters need to be ordinary and they should stay ordinary because the story demands it. Some characters are also stereotypes. We are expected to think that stereotypes are bad, however, stereotypes feature a lot in a lot of stories. Harlequin and Mills and Boon romances are centred on stereotypes: the stereotype romantic hero and heroine. The man is often of Mediterranean origin; Greek is a favourite. He is remote, arrogant and inaccessible in some way, but the plucky heroine wins him over in the end. What is wrong with stereotypes in this context? Nothing, it is what works in these stories. It is what this audience wants and expects and in this case it is what sells. If you were commissioned to write a book in this genre and did not provide what was wanted, you would be sacked.

Commedia dell'arte was a style of Italian theatre built around character types. Knowing the types enabled the audience know the world and respond appropriately. Similarly, Punch and Judy are types. We know the types, we know the stories, and we still get pleasure from watching them. If you do not have the stereotype in a work that requires the stereotypes, then editors and readers will reject it. If you pack a literary novel with stereotypes, it will be unreadable. You need to find a balance and work with your genre and reader expectations.

Write

Write as you type. Pick a style of writing you are familiar with, for example, science fiction, horror, literary fiction, fantasy or sit-com and write a brief description of a typical character type from that world. (100 words)

Flat and round characters

E. M. Forster in his classic book *Aspects of the Novel* divides the people in novels into 'flat' and 'round' characters. He says that such flat characters rarely occur in Russian novels but it would be a good thing of they did. Anyone who has read one of the classic Russian novelists will have sympathy with this view. Characters that you do not have to bother too much about, who don't change or develop through the story, are handy. We can place them in our minds as readers and they can get on with their job for the writer, which is to help with a bit of business for another character or move the plot along a little bit. We also do not need to know too much about these characters. Even if they might clamour for a bigger role, rather like an extra thinking they should be the star, your job as a writer is to keep them in their place and make sure they do the job you are paying them for. Your main characters however, your 'rounded' out characters, do need to be fully fleshed out and interesting. So let's take another tack with our shoes example and try to create a round character here.

What if we took the trainers off the feet of the student we have begun to create and put them on the feet of a 50-year-old man in a neat, dark, pinstriped business suit? What if the man was otherwise immaculately dressed in shirt, suit and tie, but on his feet were our pair of once-white, soiled trainers? What sort of picture does this give us? It is more incongruous. It is less outlandish than saying the trainers are on the feet of a 50-year-old man in a pink tutu, but it is still less expected and is potentially more interesting because of that. It does not simply complete an expected picture; it raises more questions.

Key Idea

In creating a character, do not simply complete an expected picture. Ask yourself and the character questions and leave enough gaps in the answers for the reader to ask questions.

Just as seeing a man in an airport terminal wearing one brown business shoe and one red sneaker would raise questions, so does the image of a man in a neat business suit and tie, all the usual expected assemblage of clothes, and soiled trainers. It throws off the expected picture of the businessman. We at least want to know what those shoes are doing on his feet, whereas in the other picture they belong. Having the suited man in the trainers is a more quirky picture and this also has the potential to suggest or purchase a grip on a rather less obvious character in a less obvious situation or story. Putting the dirty white trainers on the feet of this otherwise well-tailored man raises questions. The shoes do not quite fit the image. Whereas you might reasonably expect him to be wearing shoes in keeping with his outfit, polished dark shoes to go with the whole businessman's ensemble, the trainers are a surprise. And surprise is good.

 Key Idea

Surprise your readers. Let them expect the expected and then give them something else. It keeps everyone interested (you too, as you are writing).

Such surprise can raise interest value. A picture like the suited man in trainers can raise questions such as:
- How does this man come to be wearing these trainers?
- Are the trainers his?
- If so, why is he is wearing them with the suit?
- Is the suit his?
- Has he borrowed or stolen the trainers?
- Has he borrowed or stolen the suit?
- Do the trainers fit him?
- Are they someone else's trainers?
- Are they comfortable or are they pinching his toes?
- If comfortable, does that man have sore feet?

- If he has sore feet, how did that happen?
- Has he just run a marathon?
- Has he got in-growing toenails?
- Does he simply wear the trainers to travel in or to commute to work?
- Does he have his shiny business shoes in his bag or in a desk at work?

Questions, questions, questions; we have a lot of questions. Questions, like surprises, are good. While we are creating stories, characters and plots, we need to ask a lot of questions. Questions get both us and the reader thinking. And we all want thinking readers and viewers.

Any one of these questions could take us off on a different tack. If the trainers are pinching his feet, he could go some lengths to get some different ones. He might go to a shop to get some more. What if he does not have the money to pay for them? What does he do? If he has just run a marathon he might be exhausted. Perhaps he collapses, is rushed to a hospital and meets a nurse.

Key Idea

One of the hidden values of asking questions about our characters is that they raise more questions and keep our imaginations active trying to come up with the answers. A good answer should lead on to other questions and other answers, and so the process will keep growing, organically and in a fertile way.

Let's go back to our notes: what do we think about the potential character we are considering in our notebooks, the one in the suit and trainers? Is he growing a little? We are in a departure lounge at Heathrow airport waiting for the LA plane; so does he commute between London and LA? If so, what does he do? Hollywood is in LA, so does he work in Hollywood? Does he live and work in a glamorous world? We hope so, because then we may have the potential for some glamour in our story. Does he travel a lot and so know how to be comfortable, hence the trainers? But why the suit? What sort of person is capable of wearing a smart, business suit with a pair of once-white, red-laced trainers? Or plimsolls? What if the trainers were not trainers but plimsolls, or tennis shoes or old boots? What does that do to the picture?

Key Idea

Questions, questions, questions; this is the stuff of the imagination. Questions and the details of the answers are the stuff of character creation. Details, like the uniform of an army colonel or these once-white trainers, could become crucial in a story. Details can be obvious or surprising.

THE OBVIOUS VERSUS THE SURPRISING

Which would you rather have in your story: the obvious or the surprising? Let's not immediately dismiss the obvious. The obvious is good; we need it, because it sets us up for the surprising. Without the obvious, you could not have the surprising, but something that starts out in an obvious way and then stays obvious for the whole of the story would not be very entertaining or sustaining.

In life, people tend to wear items that obviously go together and which belong. It is something that we have been taught, such as 'Blue for boys and pink for girls.' There are people who make a career (certainly in television shows) out of helping people decide what to wear when, which colour suits and what goes with what. We should wear what completes the outfit; wear colours and textures that complement and do not clash. And you can do this as a writer; you can put together all the expected elements to make a complete persona or character. Hence the trainers, jeans, sweat shirt could all have come together to suggest the student character we first suggested, and a piece of writing about him could have grown quite well. But the vital thing in creating characters is that, though you start with the ordinary and need to build up a picture we can recognize, you also have to make it more than ordinary, particularly if the character is going to be important to us or is perhaps the main mover in the story. This character has to have something about them to make us want to follow them through their journey.

Key Idea

You can start to write a piece with something as simple as a pair of shoes, but you need to *build* from there. What makes these shoes different? Or, if not the shoes, what makes the person wearing them different from the expected?

Case Study: The Red Shoes

Hans Christian Anderson wrote a tale about a pair of shoes, an ordinary pair of shoes, except of course they were not an ordinary pair of shoes. They were a pair of red shoes given to a girl by a demonic shoemaker. There was a powerful obsession associated with this ordinary object which made her dance and dance till she could not stop. That tale became the basis of a classic British film, *The Red Shoes*, about a woman who sacrificed her life and love to dance and paid the price. The ordinary pair of shoes proved a demonic driver to the story.

It may not actually be the object itself that is extraordinary, as it is in the Hans Christian Anderson tale; it may instead be what the object points to or what it leads the character into. For instance, in our exercise it could be something about the man, not the shoes. We could make the man not a businessman in trainers, but something else. Perhaps on the outside he is a businessman but underneath he is really a spy or a government agent, or perhaps he may be taken for a spy because of his shoes. In fact, this idea for this story has already been done and the story has already been written.

Case Study: The Man with One Red Shoe

The Man with One Red Shoe is an early Tom Hanks film. The plot is too complicated to get into here but, briefly, the Hanks character (Richard Drew) is a composer. He has a friend, Morris, played by John Belushi who plays a trick on him by hiding one of each pair of his shoes. This means that Drew (Hanks) is forced to wear odd shoes to travel home on a flight; he wears a business shoe and one red sneaker. This is odd and unusual and some government agents think this is a code – a signal to fellow conspirators – and they begin to follow him. It leads to them searching his apartment, planting bugs to listen in on his conversations and eventually trying to assassinate him. But the key thing that sets them off in the first place is the odd shoes; the complications of plot and character stem from that. The image of someone in odd shoes is quirky; this person stands out in a crowd and that is why the agents picked the Hanks character. That is why the writer picked the device. It started us off on a character and on a story and enabled the film to poke fun at the CIA, the FBI and a host of serious 'conspiracy' films.

PLAYING WITH EXPECTATIONS

Playing with expectations in terms of the exercise we have been developing, we could have started with another sort of shoe entirely: a classy pair of shiny high-heels, for instance. What if we had a woman dressed in an ethnically patterned shirt and trousers, a beaded shoulder bag, and on her feet were not a pair of sandals as we might expect but a pair of highly polished, very high-heeled shoes. What if it was a big burly man wearing the highly polished high-heeled shoes? What sort of character and story does that suggest to us? It might suggest *Kinky Boots*, a 2005 British film in which, to quote the strapline, 'a drag queen comes to the rescue of a man who, after inheriting his father's shoe factory, needs to diversify his product if he wants to keep the business afloat'. The juxtaposition was unusual enough to be the core of an entire film.

 Write

Write a description of a man or woman where it 'all fits'; where everything goes together as expected. For example, a woman in a crisp white shirt, pearl necklace, earrings, black pencil skirt, tights and high-heeled black patent shoes carrying a black Louis Vuitton handbag. This is all of a piece. It all fits. (100 words)

Now find a way to make the description different.

As we have said, we expect people to wear clothes that are all in keeping and people generally try to do this, but how would you shake the picture of her up? How would you make the woman above different? Could you add something that would shake the picture up or give it a twist? What would that be? Think about it. Try writing it. Put her in a time and place and give this description a shake up with the addition of one single item. (150 words)

Here is another woman in brown trousers tucked into brown boots, wearing a thick-sleeved sweater on top and over that a sleeveless fur waistcoat, a bag over her shoulder, and a lime-green cell phone in her hand.

What do you make of her? Does this all fit?

Write

Try to visualize this character:

A woman in a tailored, blue, pinstriped trouser suit, silver blazer buttons down the front and a simple blazer button on each cuff.

What picture is this conjuring for you? Before you read on, stop and either think of a picture or write down on a piece of paper what this picture suggests to you. Just write one word, e.g. 'doctor' or 'chimney sweep'. Write whatever image you get. Do that now.

Let's add a bit more detail:

She also wears black shoes with mid-height heels and a white, open-necked blouse with a red scarf tucked in it.

What sort of picture do you get now? Is it growing? Does this woman work or not? A policewoman? Write down what you think. Now if we add:

She has an ID badge on a chain hung around her neck.

Does this make her more likely to be at work or perhaps at a conference?

If she is at work, what sort of work does she do? Is she a policewoman in uniform? Not with the pin stripes and the tailored look. Without being unfair to policewomen, could she be just that little bit too well turned out to be on the beat? A policewoman would probably be wearing comfortable flat shoes good for walking and she would need a leather belt for her necessary handcuffs and stick. What if we add in more detail?

Her make-up is neat and her blonde hair nicely washed and styled; her nails are well manicured and painted and she is wearing gold earrings.

No, she is not a policewoman, not one on duty anyway. Perhaps she is a lawyer? Maybe she is too well presented even for that. How about that scarf? A final bit of detail might help:

Her scarf is not in fact red, but red, white and blue. She wears a single silver wing on her lapel.

The red, white and blue scarf and silver wings reveals that she is a British Airways flight attendant. Is she in fact on duty on the 9.55 London Heathrow flight to Los Angeles where perhaps she and our character in the once-white trainers could strike up a rapport? It is a small world. Anything can happen.

Details accumulate

From this you can see how outside details accumulate to create the character and also how small details, such as the silver wing and red, white and blue scarf, can either focus the character or throw the picture off. Maybe you were not expecting the silver wing and flight attendant had not come into your mind. Maybe you were expecting something else. That's ok. If something like this comes up in a story, your readers will be happy to adjust.

Don't be afraid to throw odd elements in. As we have said, we expect people to wear clothes and carry accessories that match. If they don't, it can raise questions such as why is a man in a business suit carrying a pink phone or a lorry driver carrying a teddy bear. And remember, questions are good.

 Key Idea

Writers can and must play with expectations. We must set up expectations in the reader but we must not always fulfil them. Instead we must confound the reader's expectations and keep them on their toes.

10 TIPS FOR SUCCESS

1 *Writers can learn a lot from actors, both by the questions they ask of a piece of writing and how they approach creating parts.*

2 *You can create characters from inside out and from outside in.*

3 *An everyday item of clothing such as a pair of shoes can be the beginnings of a character and a story.*

4 *Make the ordinary quite ordinary where it needs to be and less ordinary where it can be.*

5 *Writing takes muscles. Keep exercising every day.*

6 *Don't be limited by what is true. Writers take the truth and use it to lie.*

7 *Flat, stereotypical characters serve a vital role in the right place in the right stories.*

8 *Never stop asking questions of your characters.*

9 *The wrong detail can throw a character portrait off; the right details can crystallize and bring into focus a character portrait.*

10 *Challenge a reader's expectations. Keep them on their toes.*

5

What if?

In this chapter you will learn:

- further exercises in creating characters from outside in
- about a real-life fictional character creation
- the concept of 'wallet-litter'
- the importance of asking 'what if?'

Further exercises in creating characters from outside in

Shoes, clothes, wallets, phones, all the clutter that people wear and carry are useful for writers seeking to create characters. Handbags could do a similar job to shoes in characterization.

HANDBAGS

The very style of handbag can speak volumes about the woman (or man) carrying it. It is just a bag to carry belongings in, yet handbags come in endless styles and designs and are made of so many different materials. Some have straps over the shoulder, some don't. They can be made of leather, fabric, metal, fur, beads; designers create amazingly unusual objects. Women will carry a different one for different occasions and to wear with different outfits. Seeing a woman in a no nonsense business suit carrying a bright pink handbag is an interesting picture; interesting because it immediately raises questions. The 1980s British Prime Minister Margaret Thatcher is a good historical example of 'woman with handbag'. She was rarely seen in public without her handbag. But what did Margaret Thatcher keep in her handbag? What would you keep in there if you were a woman at the top in politics? Just as the outside design, shape and style are important, so too is what is on the inside. What the bag carries can be very revealing about character and lifestyle.

Write

Look at one or two of the female characters in a story you are writing or have written and ask yourself what they would keep in their handbags. What clutter is there in there? Do the same for a man with a wallet. If you can't think of a character of your own to do this with, find a character in story you like and imagine what they have in their bags or wallets. Make a list. (150 words)

What did you learn from this? Does anything in the bag give you a new insight into the character? Can this new insight take your story off in a new direction?

Case Study: David Copperfield

There are some good examples of characters through handbags in fiction. Oscar Wilde had a handbag play a very central role in the plot of *The Importance of Being Earnest* where the eponymous hero tells us late in the action that he does not know his parents because he was left as a baby in a handbag in Victoria Station – the Brighton line.

In Charles Dickens' *David Copperfield*, David's widowed mother marries Mr Murdstone (we know that is not going to be good news; look at the name.) Mr Murdstone's sister Jane arrives to live with them. She has a handbag. The story is told through the little boy David's eyes and he sees the handbag almost as soon as he sees her. He describes it as having her initials driven into its side with nails. And as she shuts the bag, the snap makes him think it is big enough to cut his head off. What telling images. The boy's perceptions are frightened and dramatic all at once and all this is given to us through his first sight of her handbag. We see the bag as he sees it, big and hard and threatening. Dickens tells us so much about the boy and about the woman and their likely relationship by simply letting us see her and her handbag through his eyes. It would be wrong for her to have a pink frilly bag. The style of handbag goes with the picture he paints of Miss Murdstone. But though the item itself as an item of clothing is entirely fitting, Dickens also uses it brilliantly to suggest the cold, new threat that has entered David Copperfield's life. It could be very interesting for us to ask just what was in Jane Murdstone's handbag. Maybe she had something fluffy and pink inside it. She was horrible to David and certainly a woman full of Victorian iron and discipline, but she was fond of her brother and therefore capable of some feeling. The contents of a handbag could enable us to construct a character quite complex and individual.

Key Idea

Objects are more than mere description; they can reveal aspects of character and relationships. When you are giving us objects that belong with the character, don't make them all obvious, make at least one or two of them significant in some other way. Something one character takes for granted can be seen by another character as significant, dangerous or threatening or desirable in some way.

If you were able (legally) to go through different handbags in order to think about the sort of people who owned them, you would be able to construct a variety of different characters. These characters might not actually be 100 per cent the people who own the bags, but your imagination would be quickened and stirred by what you found. From tickets for a plane, a train or a cinema; from receipts and shopping lists, you can conjure up very believable pictures of someone's age, background, hair colour, of the people they love in their lives and where they've been or are going.

Write

Ask a friend or acquaintance if you can go through their bag, or if they can tell you what they have in their bag. Make a list of the items inside. If you can't find a handbag to go through with the owner's permission, use the following list:

Lipstick, hair brush, tickets for bus and train, a pen, sweets and a revolver.

What do you make of these items?

Write down your immediate sense of the character suggested. Do it now before reading the commentary below. (200 words)

The contents of a handbag

Many of the contents on the list in the exercise above are quite unsurprising. It would be worth knowing the colour of the lipstick. If it was crimson it could suggest a different image to that suggested by demure, pale pink. Is the lipstick of a colour that the woman would never wear in her day job? That would suggest a secret, other life. Then there is the revolver. Most women could be expected to have lipstick, a hair brush, tickets for bus and train, a pen, and sweets ... but a gun? This does stand out from the ordinary. Even in the United States where gun laws are such that many more people have guns, not every woman has a hand gun in her purse. This is a dangerous weapon. Is she in danger? Has she been threatened? Does she need it for protection or is she seeking someone to kill? Is it perhaps not her gun but something she borrowed from someone? Who from and why did she borrow it? Is she carrying it for a boyfriend or partner?

When you are looking for something different it can be a good idea to go for contrast again, but to stand out it does not have to be something as dramatic as a gun. As we have said, a woman dressed in a smart, dark business suit carrying a pink frilly handbag would stand out. This would be a woman either making a statement or who does not care what sort of statement she makes.

Workshop: Handbag

Describe a woman from outside, with a handbag. Give her clothes of a particular sort, e.g. a smart, no nonsense business suit or jeans and a T-shirt. Inside the handbag put eight to ten objects, one of which contrasts with the outward appearance she seeks to convey. This way you can try to give her a secret, inner life that is reflected by what is in her handbag. (200 words)

Workshop: Wallet

Repeat this exercise with a wallet for a man. Men are not able to carry such large items in their wallets so you could use the pockets of his jacket or trousers too, but still go for contrast between the appearance of the man outside and what he has in his wallet and pockets. (200 words)

The handbag/wallet exercise is a good thing to do when revising a piece of writing. It can also be incredibly useful to repeat this exercise with actual, concrete items, such as a set of keys, or a letter, or a book. It may be that you feel something is not quite working with a character; perhaps they haven't quite gelled and remain out of focus. In which case, you could make a list of what they carry in their handbag, wallet, pocket or other bags. You may in all likelihood not use all or even any of these in your piece, but the very act of thinking about them can often help you get a new insight into the character and result in you writing the character better.

Key Idea

Any extra insights you gain from exploring the 'outside' of a character can only enrich an already complex character and a make a dull character more interesting.

Case Study: Sherlock Holmes

Many details have become central to our image of the most famous detective of them all: Sherlock Holmes. He lives at one of the most famous addresses in all literature: 221B Baker Street. The 'B' in 221B is a good touch. It somehow says so much more than 221 would have done. The address '221 Baker Street' is ordinary and expected; 221B is not ordinary, it has more about it. It raises more questions, such as where is 221A Baker Street? Is the address an apartment? This was a touch brought to the character by the writer, Conan Doyle, along with the creation of Dr Watson and Mrs Hudson.

Then we have the deerstalker hat and the Inverness cape, a magnifying glass, a violin, a syringe, the meerschaum pipe. We immediately associate all of these details with Holmes and at once, through them, we know we could only be in a Sherlock Holmes story world. But interestingly, so many of the exterior details we associate with Holmes were not given by the author; they were added by others.

The deerstalker and the Inverness cape came from one of the very early illustrators in *The Strand Magazine*, Sidney Paget. He first dressed Holmes in these clothes and these are the clothes that have become stamped in our minds forever as Holmes. American actor William Gillette, who put together a stage script from several of the Holmes stories and performed it over a thousand times, further added the pipe, a magnifying glass, a violin and a syringe. This is typical of what happens when a piece of prose is adapted for the stage. Small details of character that are merely mentioned in the story need to be made concrete and real to create the character on stage. Apparently it was also Gillette who came up with the phrase: 'Oh, this is elementary, my dear fellow', which has come down to us as one of the most famous quotations in the English language: 'Elementary, my dear Watson.' This quote and these items are all archetypal Holmes. They are what stand for Holmes and a lot of them were brought to the character by people other than the writer.

Key Idea

The creation of Sherlock Holmes, the character, is like the most powerful characters of Shakespeare or Moliere, able to withstand any amount of interpretation and adding on by succeeding generations. He is so strong that he can take it all and still remain what he was. He is also a composite formed of contributions from the writer, other artists and the imagination of the public.

It is as if the readers of Holmes' stories, in order to make Sherlock Holmes more real than even Conan Dole had envisaged, seized on these details to crystallize him in the public mind. But all characters are composites of one sort or another. Let's look at a real-life fictional character creation and how the authors of this character brought him into existence.

'Wallet-litter'

Operation Mincemeat is a powerful example of using fictional techniques to create a life not on the pages of a novel or a screenplay but in the real world. It occurred during the Second World War and has been written about in several books since then. The story of Operation Mincemeat is told in detail in *The Man Who Never Was* (1953) by Ewen Montagu, and *Operation Mincemeat* (2010) by Ben Macintyre. It was also made into a film, *The Man Who Never Was*, in 1956. The heart of the plan was a deception cooked up by the British Intelligence services to fool the Germans about the proposed place for an Allied invasion in Sicily.

The Allies wanted to make the German High Command think that the invasion everyone expected to take place in Sicily would actually be somewhere else. If the deception worked, the Germans would move men and weapons to this false place and away from the real invasion point. The plan that the originators of this scheme hit on was to do exactly what a novelist or scriptwriter would do: they sought to create a fictional character from a completely plausible background to sell a story to their readers, the Germans. They wanted to use fictional techniques not to create a story or a novel, but to influence the outcome of the war and to save as many Allied lives as they possibly could. It is a brilliant story of deception in war and is fascinating to look at in terms of how the intelligence service created a person who did not exist, and a plot that was believable, and a story so convincing that it was able to directly affect the conduct of the war.

The actual plan was to drop a body into the sea where the Germans would find it. This body would need to have papers on it that would convince the Germans that the Allies were planning to invade where they were not. It had to be convincing, for if the Germans doubted it and thought it was a fabrication, then this would tell them immediately where the real invasion was to take place. The Germans had to believe the character and be fully taken in by the story that the body and the documents he was carrying with him had to tell. The stakes were very high.

It was not enough to find a dead body, attach to his arm a brief case full of (fake) top-secret documents and drop him into the sea. The details had to be right. It had to be the right kind of dead body and the documents had to be the right kind of documents. Most importantly, the fictional character had to be convincingly genuine because when the Germans checked into him, he had to have a background that would hold up. The authors of the plot thought very carefully about details that would spell out his life. In a process exactly like that of a novelist or scriptwriter, they spent a long time thinking of the right name. It was also important to decide on the right uniform to put him in and give him the right job so that he could have access to the right level of confidential information needed to trick the Germans. In the end they called him William Martin and made him a major in the Royal Marines. They attached him to Combined Operations Headquarters and gave him a wallet into which they put a genuine Combined Operations Headquarters Pass in the name of Major William Martin, such as a real major would have carried. Because this was shiny and new they marked it as a replacement card, issued to replace one that had been lost; a good touch. Losing such a pass was a serious matter and revealed something of his character. Thinking further about the sort of detail that would convince the Germans that this was a real, genuine person, they added to his character by providing him with what has come to be called 'wallet-litter': all the 'stuff' a man carries with him. They also gave him keys, a packet of cigarettes (Player's Navy cut), a watch, a box of matches and a belt. They added a bill for a Royal Marines battle dress from the military tailors Gieves of Piccadilly, dated and paid and crumpled it up in his pocket. The clothing was new so one of the authors of the plot, Charles Cholmondeley, wore them for a few months, breaking them in. He and his fellow author Ewan Montagu added a temporary member's bill for the Naval and Military Club in Piccadilly, Martin's identity card and some theatre tickets. This concentration on detail gave Martin a plausible existence, a background to come from and a story to tell, but the authors of the plot still felt that something was missing. It was important that the character they were creating did not remain just a collection of 'things'. Something had to hold them together, and that something was an inner life. As well as gathering these numerous items, they had to come up with something that animated the character they were creating, that both held it together and gave it the dynamism of a real life.

They needed to develop and round out his personal life, so they added to the 'wallet-litter', putting in items suggesting a romance: a photograph of a young woman and some letters from her, signed 'all my love, Pam'. They asked real people in the service to submit photos and got a colleague to write the letters. They also obtained a bill for an engagement ring from a Bond Street jeweller, which added to the sense of authenticity they wanted to create. To add yet more detail about his background, they obtained a very formal letter from Martin's bank manager at Lloyd's Bank demanding settlement of an overdraft and threatening consequences if he did not attend to the matter. To this they added a letter from William Martin's father which further filled in details about the family background and showed an irritation at his son's attitudes to life and money. Two identity discs stamped 'Major W. Martin R.M, R/C' showed that he was a Roman Catholic.

All their careful, imaginative work created what appeared to be a living, breathing human being who had an outer and an inner life. He was in the Marines, engaged to be married, he overspent and was being threatened by his bank. He also smoked and was a little careless. Did his story stand up?

Macintyre, in his book *Operation Mincemeat*, says that many spy novelists such as Somerset Maugham, Ian Fleming, John Le Carre, Graham Greene had had experience of intelligence work. Macintyre makes the point that novelists and spies have a lot in common, needing to create credible characters in a credible world and then to lure readers in by their craft and artifice to believe the world as true. The sorts of details of character, life and place that Operation Mincemeat used are all the sorts of details that an author would put together for any fictional character they were creating. A combination of believable details about a character's life and lifestyle, how they live and where they live are needed to make a fully fledged, three-dimensional, rounded figure. The British plot was successful and its success must have owed a good deal to the careful accumulation of detail about the personal life of the major and the world he would have come from.

Key Idea

Use detail in the characters you create; it will help you achieve the important dynamic of the inner and the outer that is essential for all rounded characters.

'What if' questions – the importance of asking 'What if?'

Major Martin was developed through a series of 'what if' questions. What if they could find a body to use? What if they could convince the Germans he was genuine? What if they dropped him into the water off Spain or France but he wasn't found? What if he was found but the French or Spanish authorities did not hand the details over to the Germans?

The time spent in the writing process creating a character full of incredibly rich and exciting 'what if' moments; moments when you can let your imagination play; moments where you can ask yourself and the character questions and feed on the answers. Some of it will stay with you and be important for your character. Much of it won't, but it is the essential sort of work that will enable you to create the characters in the first place. The more questions you raise about your characters, the more chance they have of growing and growing to be multidimensional. If the characters that appear in your writing raise questions, your readers will try to answer them. They will be engaged and active readers and viewers, not just passive receivers getting what they expected and at risk of getting bored.

Key Idea

A favourite question for a writer is 'What if?' What if the car didn't stop? What if the house burnt down? What if the couple never met? What if the mail was never received? What if the character did this instead? What if the character was a man instead of a woman?

'What if' also works for the writing process. What if you crossed that bit out? What if you moved the opening scene to later in the book? What if you lost that character and turned two characters into one?

Write

Imagine you are writing a spy story. You need to create a convincing spy. Ask 'what if' questions to help you. Then, using what has become called 'wallet-litter', put together the background story for a man or woman of your choice. (250 words)

NOTHING IS WRITTEN IN STONE

Some detail you come up with from asking 'what if' questions may support you while you are writing, but may well have to come out again as you progress. You need to get into the habit of thinking that not everything you write is necessary or will need to stay in your story. Some of what you come up with in your thinking will help you find out what it is you are writing. Some of what you write is writing on the way; it is part of the journey. You may not need it when you get there. The more you can be happy with writing something just to see how it works, and taking it out again if it doesn't work or doesn't contribute, the more confident you will be in your writing, the more you will develop the necessary fluidity of mind that allows your writing to breathe and grow.

'Nothing is written in stone,' scriptwriters and producers sometimes say. This means that just because you have written it down does not mean it has to stay if it is wrong or throwing something else off; everything is up for grabs. The practice of putting in such lines of dialogue, a piece of description, some explanatory narrative or an image or two, of testing their suitability and of taking them out again is the best way to gain confidence in your writing and of attaining mastery over what you are doing. If, when you write something, you are afraid to change a single comma, then you are not in control of your craft. The more you get used to taking it all apart and putting it back together again, the more mastery you will gain over what you do.

 Key Idea

A lot of discoveries in writing are trial and error; you do it and see if it works. If it does, then keep it; if not, put it back the way it was.

10 TIPS FOR SUCCESS

1 *Any number of items can contribute to the creation of an intriguing character.*

2 *The very act of thinking about characters' external appearance and/or possessions can often help you get a new insight into them and result in better characterization.*

3 *Ask questions of your characters. Any extra insights you gain can only enrich an already complex character and a make a dull character more interesting.*

4 *Trying to tease out a character is an ideal time to ask 'what if' questions.*

5 *'What if' questions can be used for both character and plot and can connect character and plot.*

6 *It is always a good idea to let as many ideas as you can go through your head about a character before you settle on specifics.*

7 *Writers need to create credible characters in a credible world, which lures readers in to believe the world as true.*

8 *'Wallet-litter' can tell readers a great deal about your characters and you can use it in the writing stage to help you find and form your characters.*

9 *Nothing is written in stone. Just because you have written something down does not mean it has to stay in. If it works, keep it; if it does not work, modify or throw it out.*

10 *Give your characters an inner life too and try to unite their inner and outer worlds.*

6

Surface appearance and reality

In this chapter you will learn:

- the difference between surface and reality in characters
- how to create memorable and enduring characters
- how to create characters from inside out
- about powerful character drives.

Surface appearance and reality in characters and stories

William Martin, Major Royal Marines, was created to tell a fiction to the Germans. On the surface, Major Martin was to appear one thing, in reality we know that he was something else: a plant, an ordinary man whose body was used to create Major Martin. One of the staples of thousands of stories and character construction is that mostly the surface is not what it seems and the story is spent revealing that. The fact that characters and situations can appear one thing on the surface but in reality are something else is staple fare for the spy fiction genre. It is also used a great deal in comedy and tragedy. Moliere's character Tartuffe is very much one thing on the surface and another in his heart, as is Iago in *Othello*. The action of the plays brings this out.

It is very common in stories for people and places to have more going on than appears on the surface. It is also possible to turn this around and go with the idea that there is *less* going on beneath the surface.

Case Study: The Man with One Red Shoe

The film we discussed earlier, *The Man with One Red Shoe*, plays with this difference between surface and reality. The irony with this film is a nice one in that we have a character that, beneath the surface, is exactly what he seems to be but the spies, having decided Drew himself is a spy, don't believe it. They think his surface life is a very clever cover and there has to be more beneath it. They believe what we see is not what we get and are determined to prove it. When Drew, a musician, composes a snatch of music they believe it is a code. They begin to invest so much time and energy into their central belief that he is an agent that they cannot back off and change their minds about the reality beneath the surface. They probe more and get themselves in too deep. They want something else to be beneath the surface but in this story there is nothing. The joke is that the hero is exactly what he seems to be.

 Key Idea

Giving your characters hidden agendas and secrets can give them that depth and help to make them more rounded.

DETAIL, DETAIL, DETAIL

Characters are made up of what is on the surface and what is under the surface. It is important to establish a surface reality but there has to be something underneath as well, certainly with your main characters. Two-dimensional characters can remain flat and two-dimensional. Three-dimensional characters need to be more rounded, need to have the depth that comes from being more rounded. What do we see in our characters and stories? Most immediately we see the surface. What is on the surface? Details, details, details; details such as all of the ones carefully established by the authors of Operation Mincemeat.

As we have seen, detail is crucial in character creation. What do we see when we look at the marble statue of *Samson Slaying a Philistine* referred to in chapter two? We see the two men, their hands and faces, their feet, the slave writhing beneath Samson's knee, his head yanked back, waiting for the crushing blow to be delivered from the jaw bone of the ass. We see the surface detail, the physicality of the scene, and this is what allows us to see the terror beneath. This is a moment before a killing, before death, and the artist's incredible skill and attention to detail captures this for us. We see the life and energy imbued into the stone by the artist and we can only see this by looking at and through and into the physical manifestation that the artist Giambologna offers us. It is exactly the same with the Rembrandt portraits and self-portraits we discussed. The work is made up of a physical offering, the surface reality of paint on canvas, the accurate rendition of details of costumes and clothing, of hands and eyes and skin, all done by the artist and conveyed by his brush strokes; this is what takes us through to something else – to the humanity of a human life. Writers love details.

> ## Key Idea
>
> Details are the building blocks of character creation; without details there would be no character. With *only* details there would be no character.

Creating memorable and enduring characters

Think of all the detective characters in murder mysteries that have endured. What has kept the dapper Belgian, Hercule Poirot, in the minds of readers and viewers for nearly a century? It is the detail:

the detail of his appearance, the small, neat, curled moustache and the accented English with his familiar phrase, 'the little grey cells'.

Though if this was all there was, the character would not be as powerful or have endured as long as it has done. If he were only what he is on the surface, he would not be *the* Hercule Poirot. As well as the surface detail, as well as how he is described and what we see, he has a mind and a way of acting which cuts against the surface portrait. It is the way his mind works, the manner in which he conducts his enquiries and always solves the puzzle, combined with his appearance, that lifts him into the ranks of the truly memorable characters in fiction. With someone like Poirot it can also be our growing familiarity with a character, the way we come to know him over time through an ever-enlarging oeuvre of adaptations of the stories. But if he were not a good creation in himself, no amount of familiarity would allow him to stay in our minds as he does. Ultimately it is a combination of the telling detail that the author finds to describe him, both on the surface and underneath, *and* the way the character and the plot intertwine and combine that makes him so successful and so recognizable.

Why is Columbo, another detective, so memorable? Through all the television repeats he has become very familiar to us. We know him as instantly as we know Poirot but that can't be the only reason he is memorable. Familiarity *can* breed contempt. Because we know him, we also know the world he moves in. Think of Columbo's shabby raincoat and old, battered car, and that seemingly cluttered and shambolic manner of his. These are endearing details for a character but perhaps not expected in a detective, which is exactly the point. We would want our detectives to be organized and decisive and assertive, to have authority, confidence and to be in control – the opposite of the seemingly diffident, apologetic character that we get with Columbo. The way he is presented does not lead us to expect much but, though he does not look like it, Columbo is excellent at his job. When Columbo flatters the star name in the show and calls them sir and ma'am and talks in an inconsequential way to them, when he says that he is puzzled by 'just one more thing', we know, and his opponent begins to realize, that he has put his finger on the main weakness in the murderer's alibi and that he is going in for the kill. He is a brilliant detective, but his outward appearance would suggest the opposite.

APPEARANCES CAN BE DECEPTIVE

As we've said already, writers set readers and viewers up to expect one thing, but give them another. The fact that appearances can be deceptive is what is at work here and is where the power of detail can be twisted and turned and deepened. The shabby raincoat and the apologetic manner are surface characteristics that only come into importance when contrasted with the razor sharp mind of the policeman beneath. Even when we know how it all works, as in the Columbo stories, we enjoy it. We enjoy the predictability; we enjoy how he does it. This familiarity is comforting. We know where we are. We know Colombo will always get his man or woman. Order will be restored. This comfort that readers and viewers take from the murder mystery genre should not be underestimated.

What we see with Columbo and characters like him is the working together of the inner and the outer. The outer character is a mere collection of details without the dynamism and energy of the inner mind and man. Combined they make a character dynamite.

Key Idea

Character is nothing without the dynamism of inner and outer. Find all the telling details you want in putting a character together, yet the character will remain dead if it is without wants and needs to fulfil, actions to perform and obstacles to overcome – and without a plot.

Case Study: Father Brown

The appearance and reality combination and difference has been a common way of constructing character in murder mystery fiction. When G. K. Chesterton created Father Brown he deliberately gave him a most innocuous appearance. From his face to his clothing, Chesterton made him ordinary and quite bland so that he could contrast with the sort of man he was beneath. Father Brown sees crimes where others do not. He solves them where others cannot. His outward appearance belies the acute inner man. Chesterton's little priest, unnoticed by so many in the stories, with the energy and dynamism of his inner life is, like Poirot and Columbo, one of the great detectives.

Write

Think of a character that is very good at something, for instance a virtuoso pianist or a top sports person, then write a character description in which the appearance of the character contrasts strongly with the inner life of the character. (200 words)

APPEARANCE AND REALITY IN SHAKESPEARE

The appearance and reality relationship is not just a favourite of crime or spy fiction. It is an essential device of plotting and of characterization from murder mystery to Shakespeare. As mentioned, Iago's outward appearance, combined with his smooth manner, belies the cruel, manipulative and malevolent forces within. He is trusted by everyone – Othello, Desdemona, Emilia and Cassio – and often referred to as 'honest Iago' but the true deception that is Iago is not openly revealed until the end of the play, by which time tragedy has ensued.

Key Idea

Character creation is the combination of the outer and the inner, of how a person is outside and what he is like inside. It can be very dynamic when the inner and the outer are at odds with each other.

Inner conflict

When Hamlet learns that his father did not die naturally but was murdered by his own brother, Hamlet's uncle Claudius, who has since taken the opportunity to seize the crown of Denmark and bed and wed the dead king's wife (Hamlet's own mother), Hamlet is devastated.

'O villain, villain, smiling, damned villain!' he says in Act 1, Scene 5 where he is sickened to the core by the behaviour of both his uncle and his mother.

> *O most pernicious woman!*
>
> *O villain, villain, smiling, damnèd villain!*
>
> *My tables—meet it is I set it down*
>
> *That one may smile, and smile, and be a villain—*
>
> *At least I am sure it may be so in Denmark.*

Hamlet sits exactly at that point of discord between appearance and reality, between what we can call the outer and the inner worlds. 'That one may smile, and smile, and be a villain.' That someone can be one thing on the surface and quite another underneath seems amazing to him, but then Hamlet is a young man.

This discord between the inner and the outer has been much used in tragedy and comedy. It is the same discord as between the bumbling, out of his depth surface appearance of a detective like Columbo and the reality of the brain beneath that will snap shut like a razor-sharp trap on the murderer. What is on the surface, what we see, what is outer is not the always truth and is often at odds with what is inside.

Key Idea

As writers, what makes our characters more real, interesting and complex is an ability to move between outer and inner, appearance and reality; between what is said and what is thought or felt and what is done. We have to be able to imagine and to write the inner as well as the outer and to create situations in which this relationship can be tested and the tension made manifest for the reader and viewer.

CREATING WHOLE CHARACTERS

The gap between the outer and the inner has been explored continually in stories throughout time. It should be explored in the writing you are going to produce. You need to be able to create characters with surface verisimilitude and inner depth, and in a very good story the two will be at odds with each other. The gap between what they appear and what they are, between what they say and what they really mean, between what they do and what they really do, all these are what can contribute to make these characters whole as well as more memorable and significant and stand out from the crowd. This is what a story and a plot should aim to bring out. This can be made manifest in what characters do, the actions they take and are compelled to take in a story.

Both heroes and villains in our stories, if they are to be central and substantial characters, need to have more going on than appears on the surface. We must remember that characters may do and say one thing but think and be something else beneath; they may want something but need something else. This is where a real tension in both character and story can come from. If we can, we must therefore establish a surface life for a character and another life or another layer or a deeper series of wants, needs and ambitions beneath that surface.

So, as well as establishing characters from the outside we need to know what our characters are like from within. How do we do this? There are two considerations here:

1 **How do we understand what our characters are like inside?**

2 **How do we get this across in our writing?**

Case Study: Sherlock Holmes

We looked at the outer appearance of the great detective Sherlock Holmes; let's continue now by looking at Holmes from within. What makes Holmes unique?

Holmes and Columbo are in some ways very different and in others the same and comparing them also shows, incidentally, how far the idea of the 'detective' has travelled. Where Columbo just about upholds the traditions of the great detective, shambling and scruffy and apparently chaotic and with authority almost in spite of himself, Holmes is sharp and organized with a natural authority. Even though he is just as much a commoner as Columbo, Holmes also has an aloof, almost aristocratic manner which puts him on a par with aristocrats. Holmes' intellect and above all his authority over his subject even raise him up beyond this level.

Columbo is a most democratic cop and he works at a time when authority has been largely undermined. Holmes came from a time when authority was highly respected. His manner of proceeding derives a good deal of its form and authority from the medical profession. Conan Doyle had been trained and practised in the respected profession of a doctor and he began to write Sherlock Holmes stories sitting in his consulting room waiting for patients. In his life he was a doctor, he thought like a doctor, and when it came to his writing and to creating the character of Sherlock Holmes, he naturally drew on his knowledge and training in the medical profession. What else would be expected? When lawyer John Grisham began writing thrillers, he wrote about lawyers. Michael Ridpath used his background as a bond trader in the city of London to create a thriller involving a bond trader in the city in his novel *Free to Trade*, which earned him huge advances when it first appeared. Dick Francis, once a jockey, turned to writing thrillers set in the world of horse racing.

 ## Key Idea

All writers draw on their experience and knowledge, then make up the rest.

Colin Watson in his book on crime fiction, *Snobbery with Violence*, shows how Doyle made use of his medical background in creating the character of Sherlock Holmes. Holmes, a consulting detective, is often found in his consulting rooms waiting for clients. Holmes interviews clients rather like a consultant doctor would, probing for clues to the client's sickness. He often has to think a long time about the problem before doing some exploratory work and before offering a diagnosis. Holmes is more than averagely intelligent, he is loyal to the Crown and a fierce patriot, he can be rude and brusque but in so many ways is admirable. Contrast this with his weaknesses, for cocaine, for his pipe and with the fact that he has a bruised heart from an encounter with an 'unparalleled' female criminal, and you have a complex character with a mixture of conflicting or incompatible characteristics. On the surface he is intelligent, arrogant and self-sufficient, but beneath this there is weakness and insecurity and emotional doubt. Doyle certainly did not make Holmes flat and two-dimensional.

Write

Write a piece in which a character is at odds with themselves. Find ways to show their inner struggle. The struggle may be to do with work or with a relationship. Perhaps they are privy to a piece of knowledge and are in a quandary about whether to share it with another character. What do they do and say as they struggle with this dilemma? Plunge them into a situation that brings this out. (500 words)

Creating characters from inside out

We have said quite a bit about description and external details, but what of the inner life? How do you reveal a character's inner life?

This is sometimes easier to do in prose where you can take a reader into the narrative and share with them what a character is feeling and thinking, their thought processes as they sense and think and respond. The stream of consciousness technique, pioneered by Henry James and developed by writers such as James Joyce and Virginia Woolf, aimed at imitating the inner life, seeking to show us all the tiny changes in a person's thoughts by clipping syntax, by letting ideas overlap, by allowing us to share the teeming inconsequentiality of much of what purports to be the inner workings of our minds.

Revealing a character's inner thoughts is harder to do on stage or on screen. The problem here is that, for anyone to apprehend it, the inner life has to be made visible or audible. If someone stands on stage saying and doing nothing other than thinking, it is hard for the audience to know what they are thinking; they could be thinking anything. Film and television actors sometimes believe they are conveying all sorts of emotions through the minute changes on their faces, and sometimes they are. Some actors can wonderfully convey the change from one thought to another with a movement of the mouth, a flicker in the eyes. Others fail. We know they are trying to convey a thought or an emotion, but we are not sure what it is. Some actors fall back on a look they do to camera, a vacant look that it is up to the audience to fill in. In some actors, grief or love can look like indigestion!

 Key Idea

Films and plays have to show inner life through outer means. They have to make what is invisible visible.

How do films and plays do this? Dress, appearance and clothes can be a way into the inner life. A person's beliefs have an outward manifestation in the way they choose to dress, in the religious icons they choose to display in their homes or in the way they otherwise observe the rituals of their religion, but to make the invisible visible when we are writing scripts, we really have to give the characters thoughts to think, and very importantly, lines to say and actions to perform.

Let's look at something like someone's religious beliefs. A person's religious beliefs are something inwardly held, so how do we show the inner life of a religious person in a story? You can start by asking 'what if' questions about a character's religious beliefs:

- What if their beliefs are firmly held?
- What if their beliefs are not firmly held?
- What if their beliefs are held at the character's deepest core and they have absolute conviction that they are right?
- What if they are subject to grave doubts?
- What if they merely pretend to be religious for other motives?

Asking these and other questions can help you know and write the character, but how do you convey this to the reader? As we've said, it can be told very effectively in narrative or you can use the stream of consciousness technique, such as can be found in *A Portrait of the Artist as a Young Man* and *Ulysses* by James Joyce, Samuel Beckett's trilogy *Molloy, Malone Dies*, and *The Unnamable*, Albert Camus' *The Fall*, Sylvia Plath's *The Bell Jar*, J. D. Salinger's *Catcher in the Rye* and many others.

But, whether you work as a novelist or script writer, if you want to take us into the inner life and allow us to share the experience of the character's faith, doubts, fears and joys, rather than just tell us about them, the best way to do that is to put the character into some sort of situation that will bring this out. You need to write a scene or series of scenes in which we can see the character express their religious beliefs. In these scenes you could demonstrate if they observe the rituals of religious belief with full conviction or emptily, in a superficial or even social way. This way you could allow the reader to know whether the characters get themselves seen going to church because they believe it is the right thing to do or because they really wish to go. The reader can see them struggle and face up to any doubts and fears they have. If you challenge the character to look and speak and think, by having other characters act upon them, the essential inner life of something as difficult to characterize as their religious beliefs will come over to the reader and watcher through the character's external behaviour.

Write

Write a piece about a character with conviction. This character holds this belief or set of beliefs fixedly. It might be a religious conviction or it might be a conviction that a certain football team is the best in the world. Show this conviction in a scene of conflict with one other character who does not share this belief. Perhaps they worship a different god or football team. Use action and dialogue. (500 words)

Case Study: The Power and the Glory

Graham Greene's 1940 novel *The Power and the Glory* is centred on the character of a Catholic priest in Mexico at a time when the Catholic Church was outlawed and priests were being hunted down. The nameless priest at the heart of the novel has many demons. He is a 'whisky-priest' – an alcoholic who many years before also fathered a child. He is pursued by a dedicated but nameless Lieutenant. Greene puts the priest into many situations that test him to the core. He is a very ordinary human being full of human frailties. Building towards the final scenes, through his challenges, he arrives at his death in more of a state of holiness than he was at the start of the novel. And Greene does not just tell us about the man's inner struggle, we experience his struggle with him. The fact that he is a fugitive running from certain death gives the character and the narrative an imperative that takes us deep into the trials of the man's soul. The Catholic priest with all his weaknesses, doubts and fears is hunted down in a manner that tests his courage and his beliefs in the most fundamental, life-threatening ways and which directly lead to a reconciliation of the opposing forces within him. What happens is that the plot works on the character in a way that makes visible what would otherwise be unknown to us.

 Key Idea

Action and dialogue are crucial for revealing character on stage and screen. They are essential within prose stories too.

Powerful character drives

Love: the desire for it, the absence of it or the avoidance of it is a powerful drive in life. It can also be a powerful character drive. In fact it is no surprise that it has been one of the most powerful drives in films and literature.

In creating a character suffering the effects of love we could also ask the same sorts of questions we asked about a character's religious beliefs:

- What if a character sincerely believes they are in love?
- What if the character always wants to be in love?
- What if the character needs to be in love, the way they need air?
- What if their love is returned?
- What if their love is not returned?
- What consequences flow from either situation?
- What if they have been hurt by love in the past?
- What if they have they been so badly hurt that they have closed up in pain and seek to live with a determination never to feel or show love again?
- What if they have hurt a string of people and are due for a comeuppance?
- What if they are fearful and run away from love?
- What if they are still in love with someone who has left them or has died?

Some of these questions prompt ideas about character and some of them immediately lead on to ideas of situation and plot.

Love can feed desire, or grow from desire. Love can feed revenge, hurt, pain and grief and many more emotions. The love might be requited or unrequited, as for instance in Thomas Hardy's *Far From the Madding Crowd*. It can be a force for good; it can be a force for evil. It can also lead to strong characters and lead us into developing plots and stories. A character that needs love like they need air is going to try very hard to get love or to keep it. They will generate situations that beget other situations and that can lead on to fully developed plots. If you can write scenes that show this, you will bring this inner drive into the outer world of your work.

Write

Write a paragraph or two about a character who needs love or seeks to avoid love. Just write and see what comes. (300 words)

Case Study: Love in Chekhov

Love plays a huge part in many of the stories and plays of Anton Chekhov, in terms of both the characters and the plots. Characters in these stories are quite often in love with people who do not love them. In a story like *The Kiss* the narrative allows us into the head of the central character, a bespectacled officer named Ryabovitch, to experience it with him. Ryabovitch, who is at a soirée in a strange house, is kissed by an unknown woman who rushes up to him in a darkened room. Saying 'At last!' she kisses him, then stops, realizing he is not the man she thought he was. She runs off. Ryabovitch is stunned, amazed and curious. Returning to the gathering he scans the women present, wondering who it was. He does not know it at the time, but this is an incident that is going to affect him profoundly.

How does Chekhov convey to us that the character is now in love? How does he paint for us the change in the inner state of this character? He does it the only way he can, through its outward manifestation in physicality. He tells us how the character's heart was beating fast and that his cheek still carried the tingling sensation of her lips on it. He tells us how he wanted to run into the garden, to laugh, to dance, to talk out loud. He tells us how he physically wanted to let out the surge of emotion in him. Chekhov made the emotions concrete, by outward means, through what the character can see, hear, touch, smell, taste. Love, like happiness, like hope, like triumph, remains an empty, abstract notion until it is filled with such concrete detail as Chekhov supplies in *The Kiss*.

The Kiss continues with Ryabovitch in a kind of dream. He spends time trying to relive the moment of that kiss, trying to stay in that world. At the end of the story he returns to the house, the scene of the mysterious kiss, and reality breaks in and shatters the dream. He stands before a river he stood beside earlier in the story and this time his mood is entirely different. Whereas before he felt in love and special, the sense of being in love, the specialness of his sensations has by the end of the story gone completely. The same river is still there flowing into the same sea, but he now sees it differently. He sees the house and the kiss in this new, different light too. It has all become again ordinary and he misses its specialness. He sees the external scene through the spectacles of his internal mood but, this time, the same scene looks different.

Write

Write a scene about someone feeling a strong emotion, such as hate, jealousy or love. Set it in a place and time. Do not say the word hate, jealousy or love, do not tell us how they feel, but show it through the way they behave, what they think and feel and what they say. (200 words)

Write

Take the scene you have just written and write it in a different way. Where you wrote one emotion, now write the opposite. For example, where you wrote about someone in love, write about someone in hate. Keep as close to the original as you can; use the same setting, the same character, the same situation. Again do not say the words, but convey the sense of their mood through concrete detail. (200 words) What difference did this make? Did either the scene or the character change?

Key Idea

In writing you need to put your characters into situations that will allow their inner needs, desires, loves and passions to become known. We can only know if someone is in love if we share their thoughts or see them doing and saying what people in love say and do.

In the next chapter we will look at the world the character comes from: the setting.

10 TIPS FOR SUCCESS

1 *Appearances can be deceptive (thank goodness for characters and stories).*

2 *A place or a character's surface reality can be at odds with what they really are.*

3 *Details are the building blocks of characters.*

4 *Detail, however interesting and well observed, is just detail if a character has no life.*

5 *Characters are made up of what is on the surface and what is beneath the surface.*

6 *A combination of both inner and outer is what helps us create whole characters.*

7 *Character is empty without the dimension of an inner life.*

8 *Love and religion make powerful character drives. You can seek out others then create characters from them.*

9 *We can only know if someone is in love if we share their thoughts or see them doing and saying what people in love say and do.*

10 *If you want to take us into the inner life and allow us to share the character's experiences, make a scene of it.*

7

Character and setting

In this chapter you will learn:
- about creating character through setting
- how to reveal a character's inner life through place
- the importance of objects and setting
- to turn places into plot.

Creating character through setting

Just as someone's dress and the objects they possess can strongly suggest a character, so can where they live or come from – their setting.

Read the following passage.

He walked up the steps cutting the steep lawns, past signs to the library and the Schoenberg music block till he found the spot, the walkway between the library and another building. The walkway was lined with cypress trees and cast iron street lamps with glass bulbs on top to illuminate the path at night. They were unlit now except by the quiet glow which came from the daylight resting in them. He wondered what light they gave at night particularly how dark and safe this walkway was. He walked up and down the walkway twice, looking very carefully from side to side and behind each bench and cypress tree then stopped and sat on a flat stone bench next to some scattered peanut shells. They lay broken open by something human or something rodent like, a squirrel or a rat.

For a while he sat quietly alone under the unlit lamp. It was not a busy spot, not where people passed unnecessarily, not a place to meet by accident. So what had she been doing here? Suddenly a man came by in jeans and baseball cap, carrying coffee in a Styrofoam cup. A workman, he guessed, as the man receded in his denim shirt and jeans, a black belt on his waist holding tools, gloves tucked into the back pocket of his jeans like his own dad did on the golf course. A noise from the right made him turn his head. Another young man in trainers, white socks and check shorts; then from the left a girl in flop flops, flask in hand. They were all going somewhere. Rucksack on her back the girl hurried on her way. Then it was quiet again and no-one came for a while.

Had the missing woman sat there waiting like this? Had she looked up expectantly at the rushing sound of someone approaching like he had done? At that time of night, the last reported sighting of her, it would have been dark. What was she doing here? Meeting someone? Who? Where now the morning sun was making long shadows from the cypress trees in stripes across the red brick and stone flag pattern of the walkway, who would have come up the path? On this side of the path the red brick building was in shade. The library building on the other side was bright in sun. The steady glow picked out the patterns in the brick, the predominating red broken with patterns of cream stone. The library had been her favourite place to sit and work. She was logged as having been in that building that night. His eyes followed the cream stone up the walls, the cream diamonds and windows with carved cream stone arches at the top. Had she been sitting working at a desk behind one of those windows, looked up, seen someone waiting and come rushing down here? But she had been seen by the witness sitting here on this very bench alone, so had it been a prearranged meeting? Above the roof, the sky was blue; the clouds were thin and high. It was the sort of day in which you might wish to fly; to fly, to fly away. It was not possible for him to fly anywhere. Not with his workload. Ten minutes sitting here was like an oasis in his day and he was glad of it.

The buzz of an engine broke his thoughts, and then the throb of a helicopter near then distant, then more noise on the path. Three more people hurried past separately. The last was a young man in a check shirt and a woolly hat who walked with long strides away past the stone benches that were all still unoccupied except for this one.

He watched the three disappear; if they had seen him they did not appear to have noticed. Nor did they appear to have noticed the red brick path on which they'd walked. They'd probably walked it a hundred, a thousand times before and later today and tomorrow would do so again. Why would they notice it now? Why would they notice him crouching down beside it? Why did he notice them? It was his first time there so he was seeing it all with the eyes of a first time visitor. But it was more than that. He was a man who noticed things. He was one who observed, who saw and who thought. His years of training had helped with that, but he had been like that when he was their age, younger, when he was just a child he had seen and watched and thought. He had watched his parents laugh and quarrel and make up. An only child he had always been looking and listening for changes in the emotional temperature. That was one thing he was particularly good at. He could spot a quarrel at a hundred paces. But the people who went rushing past this place had places to get to and they rushed on by and did not stop. But he saw. Then he heard a nervous laugh. Looking up quickly he half expected to see the missing girl his head was so full of thoughts of her, but it was another girl rushing past. Not her. It would probably never be her. How could it, he thought, as he examined the dried blood he had just found in one of the ridges between the bricks. The hairs on the back of his neck had stood up. He knew for absolute certain now that this was not only the last place she had been seen but where she had died; where she had been murdered.

Write

Now you've read the excerpt above, consider these questions:
- What do we have here?
- Who is waiting and looking?
- Who are the people going by?
- Where are they?
- What has happened?
- Did the piece draw you in? Yes, or no and why?
- Could you carry this piece on? Try it. See where it goes. Write it before you read the analysis below.

Revealing inner life through place

Consider the questions from the exercise above:

What do we have here?

- We have a setting with several people passing by and one character not passing but standing, sitting, observing and thinking. We have a character in a place, and the character has an inner life.

What kind of place is it?

- We are not actually told what the setting is but we are given clues enough to get our minds working. The sun is out, there are shadows, the sky is clear and blue and a man wearing shorts and a girl in flip-flops pass so we know it is sunny. There is a red brick path on which people are regularly passing, going places. It is a regular route for the passers-by, though it is not too busy a place. The path is lined with benches and cypress trees and is a walkway between cream and red-coloured brick buildings. There is a library and also the Schoenberg music block. Perhaps it is a college campus and the passers-by are off to their classes. It is morning so if it is a campus, perhaps most students are in their classes.

What do we learn about the main character?

- There is no description of him from outside, we know nothing of what he looks like, nor do we know his age or his build. But we are told some facts about him: that he is a newcomer; that it is his first time there; that he was an only child and that he is observant about people and places. We are also told that he has been trained in looking and thinking. What sort of person is trained in looking and thinking? Military personnel, psychologists, writers, doctors – very many people are trained in skills like that, but what of this character?

What do we learn about him and what he is doing from inside?

- We are taken into his world by being taken into his head. We share his thoughts and perceptions; what he thinks about and what he sees. We are told that he notices things. We see him notice people passing, the layout of the place and so on and we are told that he is in the habit of looking and thinking like this.

What other clues do we get? What does he see? What subjects are coming to mind for him? How do we learn about him from inside?

- We share his thinking and see him scrutinizing the passing people and the place so we learn about his interior life. He wonders if this is a dangerous, isolated place as people do not go by all the time. It looks okay in daylight but he wonders what it might be like at night. He is also concerned over a missing young woman. Those are the sorts of thoughts a policeman could have. We learn that he is thinking of a young woman who is associated with the place. As he soaks up the atmosphere of the place and studies the people who go by, he is still but he is not passive. He sits and soaks up the sense of the place, so we as readers are able to as well. But though he is physically still and not rushing around, his mind is working. He looks and thinks and tries to imagine, as we do as readers. So though he sits and thinks, he is not passive or inert. There is movement in the piece: the movement of his mind as he tries to understand the place and potentially what might have happened there.

What does he do to reveal character?

- He walks up and down the path looking behind each bench and tree and towards the end of the section he sits down. He watches people closely, he searches the benches and trees and he gets down on his hands and knees and finds signs of blood. He has a sense that someone has been killed there and that this points to murder.

This could be the beginning of a piece, of a story or a novel. It could be about the disappearance and apparent murder of a young female student and this setting could well be crucial to the story that might unfold. The details are enough to take us in and orientate us, to begin to tell us where we are. We get the description of the red brick path and the sense of people using it to go places. It is a regular route they take.

Several people pass but at this stage they are not our focus; we are not involved with them. We may be later, but at this stage, who knows? Perhaps the man with the tools or maybe the girl with the rucksack will come back into the story shortly. At the moment they are merely passers-by. But there *are* two important characters: one present and one present in her absence; the one observing, and the young woman who is the focus of his attention.

Do you like this man? Do you know enough to decide? We know that he notices people, he is observant, he is thoughtful. He does not appear to judge the people walking by. He seems to care about what he is doing and the young woman who is missing. She has possibly been murdered here in this place. This appears to be a discovery that was not known at the start of the scene. The man discovers it through the action of the scene. This is the moment he discovers it and because he discovers it in our presence, we share it with him. This is a major discovery, it is a possible murder, and clearly will be important. Because we discover it, the discovery should become very important to us. Because he discovers it, he should now become very important to us. We are not just sitting back and watching it, we are now involved and involved with him. We could well begin to like him but perhaps we need the piece to go on to let that judgement form.

The discovery of blood and the potential for a murder kicks this story off. Discovering this is something that makes us impressed with him. He is a man who knows; he has found out and others before him possibly have not. If we see him struggle to overcome obstacles and try to discover what has happened to this young woman, we will have the chance to like him more.

What is this character's drive? He wants to know. He wants to find this young woman and if he can't find her alive he wants to find her body and discover what happened to her and bring whoever murdered her to justice. These are the powerful drives at the heart of murder mystery stories. They are strong drives and must be a lot of the reason that such fiction sells in the vast quantities it does.

If this is the start of a story, then we are immediately involved. We want to know more. More about the place, more about the missing woman, more about the viewpoint character, more about what is going on, and what has gone on, and what will be done about it.

Write

Write a piece where the setting allows a character to be introduced to us. Find something for the character to do and build the piece around an action. They can interact with others or not, as you wish, but at the end of the piece something must have been discovered and we need to share the moment of discovery with the main character. (300 words)

Just as we said that characters are not always what they seem, so it is with place. In a story a place can start out looking like it is one thing, generally friendly and hospitable, but in reality turn out to be something else.

Numerous otherwise ordinary, even idyllic, houses moved into by unsuspecting characters turn out to harbour ghosts or poltergeists or have strange pasts that work on the present to affect the lives of the characters involved. The Bates Motel never looks that inviting but it is quite a banal, rundown place for the gruesome goings on depicted in the film *Psycho*. The hotel in the 1980 Stanley Kubrick film *The Shining*, based on Stephen King's novel of the same name, is inhabited by ghosts and exerts a fatal pull on the characters. Stepford, the Connecticut town setting for the 1975 film *The Stepford Wives* (re-made in 2004) and based on Ira Levin's book, seems on the surface a most idyllic place, but that is not so beneath the surface veneer. Dracula's house in Transylvania turns out to be a very strange place, as does the house in the story *Woman in Black* by Susan Hill, which was adapted into a long-running stage play.

Write

Write a description of a place which on the surface is one thing but in reality has a very different character or purpose. Hint at the difference, suggest it, but do not overtly say what it is. (300 words)

Objects and setting

We all find handling objects that real people own very evocative. It can bring them strongly back to us. It is why people treasure letters and objects that famous people have touched, and also why rooms that people have occupied are hallowed, as if something of the person has been transmitted into the place. Could this possibly be the impulse behind establishing museums for famous people when they die? We want to commemorate and keep the famous person alive for us and the way we seek to do it is through a museum of their house and belongings. It is as if the rooms a person inhabits and the objects they touch have a certain imprint, retain a sort of energy after they have gone. It is an energy associated with that person and we want to keep that energy alive with us. When we are creating characters, we want to capture that energy and get it down on the page so that readers can share it too.

Sometimes people in grief do not wish to change the room that belonged to a person they have lost. A parent who has lost a child or a husband or wife who has lost a partner want to keep it exactly as it was the moment the lost person left it. This is partly because they hope the person might just walk back in; it is partly denial. But it is also the recognition that a place where a person lives is a most powerful source of their personality, of them. In this place the person in grief can feel still close to that person. It is as if they have not gone.

Where we live and the sorts of items we have around us can define us, can in many ways *be* us. Where else do we live but in the places we inhabit and the objects we touch, in what we say, think and do? A museum is a memorial to a person who has lived their life and now moved on, and the best memorial we can give to someone we cherish is to try to keep them alive with us, for us or for them. Whatever the reasoning behind it, we try to do this by attempting to recreate a sense of them through objects, clothes, and places they have known and that have known *them*. The lives of famous people that we as visitors somehow experience in museums are obviously not the lives of the real people that the museum has been established for; how could they be? The famous people do not actually come alive any more than a character in a book really comes alive. How could they? They are a creation, a recreation in much the same way that we create a character in a story – and they are recreated in the museums in much the same way as a fictional character is created.

In museums, the use of actual objects the famous person touched or used is often supplemented by incorporating period furniture for the rooms: wall hangings, pictures, beds. These can all persuade us when we visit that this recreated world was the world the person inhabited and allow us to imaginatively enter it. As visitors we are invited into this world in much the same way readers or viewers are invited into the world of a novel or story or film. Through putting together actual objects that the person touched, spectacles or shoes or hats they wore, books they used, books and letters they wrote, photographs and so on with period pieces that are very similar to items they might have used, a picture is created that, once injected with our imaginative juices, somehow brings that person closer to us, even *to life* for us. This is no different from creating a character on the page from real and observed details combined with imagination.

Standing in the rooms a real person once inhabited, moving about them like that person, ducking your head to go through small doorways, built for shorter people, all can give a sense that you are sharing, for an instant, that person's life. If you walk the floors of the apartment in the *Maison de Victor Hugo* in the Place des Voges in Paris, where Victor Hugo, author of *Les Miserables* lived for 16 years, you get a sense of the great writer moving past the tall windows where outside now children shriek and play in the school playground and, beyond that, the sounds of the city rumble and grumble. Revolution would have been close with all its energy and danger feeding into the writer and the man. If you visit the small house in Chawton, Hamsphire where Jane Austen lived and worked on some of her most famous novels, it is now clearly a museum. There is an entrance where you buy your tickets, there are curators to explain what is laid out for you, but walking about the narrow corridors from room to room where outside sunlight plays on the garden; seeing on display some of her letters and her music books in which pieces have been transcribed in her own hand; seeing some jewellery and a patchwork quilt that she made; marvelling at her very small writing table, close to the creaky door which she would not have fixed because it alerted her to any possible interruptions; walking to the small church as she would have walked, past the fritillaries and coltsfoot; here you can for some brief moments come close to something of the existence of this great writer.

A person's own handwriting, the place where they once sat and worked, the very spectacles they wore on their face; a piece of paper on which they wrote; Ben Franklin's glasses, George Washington's wooden teeth, Beethoven's ear trumpet... these are the sorts of items that take us near these people and that can bring them alive for us. They are hugely evocative, personalized objects that allow us to bring that person alive for brief seconds in our minds. These are the objects we need to find and put in our writing. This is not to suggest that you create a museum for your character; it is simply to say how potent the techniques of fiction are because when we want to recreate a person's life in a museum we use those techniques.

'People are places and places are people,' John Braine says in his very good book *Writing a Novel*. The National Trust, which now owns Bateman's, the seventeenth-century house where Kipling lived and wrote, exhorts us to 'soak up the atmosphere in his book-lined study'. You can stand there marvelling at his large desk. Not many miles away in Chartwell you can stand marvelling at the desk of another great man, Winston Churchill, laid out with books, papers and a telephone that was spoken into by the great man. So potent can these places and objects be that visiting these museums we can get quite a sense of the person, even years after their death. We must try to capture this potency in the settings for our stories.

Key Idea

Everyone lives somewhere; that somewhere is what we need to capture on the page if we are to give our characters a place to live; really live.

Write

Imagine you have the task of putting together a museum of someone famous. First of all, decide who they are and what they are famous for. You could do this for a real or fictitious person. If there is a real person you think should have a museum dedicated to them, then use them as the basis; if not, make someone up. Why do they warrant a museum? What sort of museum would it be? Where would it be? What would you have in it? Who would come and see it? Is there universal support or some opposition? Using the 'what if' model, create your museum. (500 words)

Case Study: The Sherlock Holmes museum

There cannot in fact be many museums created for fictional characters, but there is one. As precise and methodical as Sherlock Holmes was in his methods, Watson tells us, in a story called *The Musgrave Ritual*, that in his home Holmes was one of the most untidy men who ever lived. The chambers that he and Watson shared were piled high with stacks of papers relating to old cases and were always full of chemicals and chemical relics that ended up in the butter dish and other undesirable places. Holmes keeps his cigars in the coal-scuttle, his tobacco in the toe end of an old Persian slipper, and his letters pinned to the very centre of his wooden mantel piece with an old jack-knife. He was also not averse to indoor shooting, once sitting in his armchair taking an old pistol and a box of old boxer cartridges and carving out a patriotic VR for Victoria Regina in bullet holes. The detail of this description has proved a boon to creators of the Sherlock Holmes museum in London because it has allowed an accurate, almost realistic recreation of these rooms. When you walk round them you have to keep reminding yourself that Holmes was not actually real. It is an odd sensation but so powerful is the creation of Sherlock Holmes that it seems to many as if he did live and lives still. The boundaries between the real and the fictional have become blurred here. They have become a little blurred too in some factual books and documentaries. Television documentaries frequently dramatize their subjects now to try to make them more interesting for their audience. Writers of factual works, for instance historians, use fictional techniques these days to make their history a gripping narrative full of fascinating characters.

Key Idea

People are places and places are people. Settings suggest character. Different settings can suggest different characters.

Places into plot – a tale of two settings

Something you need to think about in your writing is: what part does environment or the setting play in your story? How does it influence – even shape – character and plot?

Write

Notes from a writer's notebook:

- 'January – a Spanish-style house in California with red tiled roofs. Bougainvillea and trailing geraniums flowering outside the door. Pines and eucalyptus growing from the dry earth and the flowering ice plants around the lawns. Bright blue pacific shining through the trees. Sunset falling over the beach. Racoons rummaging in the azalea bushes and taking night time dips in the blue pool. Owl hooting at four o'clock in the morning. Drive in an open topped car. Surf pounding in on the beaches at Del Mar. People driving by in open topped BMW sports cars past the country club where the manager greets guests by saying "welcome to another day in paradise."

- 'January – a small house in the Sussex Downs, England. Mist rolling in across the valley bottom. Sheep in the mist on the Downs and thick, slow rain falling, drenching the leafless oak trees. Wood stacked in a log store at the back of the house. Wood smoke scenting the air and foxes rooting in the dust bins at midnight.'

Using the material you have here, write a piece that compares these two settings, a house in California and a house in Sussex, England. Let your writing suggest characters, incidents, whatever comes. Ask questions like:

- Who lives there?
- What do they do?
- How are the people in these two worlds connected?

(400 words for each setting)

These two settings in the exercise above should have set up certain expectations in you. Maybe one of those was that they would be inhabited by different people. Did you write it that way? That is perfectly reasonable, though another way to do it would be to say they are owned by the same people and lived in at different times of the year. And maybe these people behave differently and feel different when they are in California to when they are in England. They may perform many of the same actions; walk the dog on the beach or on the downs; sit by the pool in California and by the fire in Sussex, eat at the restaurant on the beach, have Sunday lunch at the local pub. Outwardly the lives may be different but inwardly how are they different?

What did you do with the setting? The grey light of one place perhaps could contrast with the bright blue light of the other. The fact that California is warmer maybe suggested more of an outdoor lifestyle. In England in January it is cold and misty. People dress to keep out the cold, so it would be reasonable to expect people to behave differently in one place or the other. They would probably live life at a different rhythm, yet even though we would expect different stories, they might not be so different.

 Key Idea

Sameness and difference: people and places may well be different but also the same.

Each place might have a different surface appearance, and the job of the writer would be to convey these surfaces well so that we as readers feel we know or could know that place, but also, underneath the surface, the desires and needs of the characters may not be so different. The writer's job would be to get in there and reveal that too. A story can look very different on the surface, but the writer cannot let the story stay on the surface.

Key Idea

The surface is always a good place to start, but any writer wants to dig deeper and get below the surface in forming both characters and plot.

It could make for a good start to a story to compare and contrast two places such as this. They essentially make two worlds and many films and stories are built around this sort of idea.

Case Study: Other worlds

Two women swap their homes and their lives in Los Angeles and Surrey at Christmas in *The Holiday*, written, produced and directed by Nancy Meyers. The novel *A Tale of Two Cities*, by Charles Dickens, is famously set in London and Paris. Mark Twain's The *Prince and the Pauper* is a story where two people change lives, a prince and a pauper. In fact, taking a character from one world and putting them into another world is one of the staple ingredients for constructing stories. Alfred Hitchcock liked to take a character from one world – a mundane ordinary world that he established at the start of the film – and plunge them into another, usually involving deceptions, thrills and danger. The way the character reacts, the reactions and incidents thus generate a story, as in *North by Northwest*. In *Shadow of a Doubt* he reversed the process, first establishing the ordinary world very clearly and carefully and then introducing the dangerous, different element of Uncle Charlie, the murderer, into that environment.

There are stories with people swapping bodies, where one person inhabits the body of someone else and has to deal with the issues that that causes. This is not dissimilar to people moving from one world to another. In fact *other worlds* is quite a common theme and setting in many stories. It does not have to be science fiction and aliens, or ghost stories and haunting as in the film *The Others* or in the clever cult movie *The Sixth Sense* in which Bruce Willis plays a psychologist trying to help a young boy who claims he can see dead people. People can shift and change worlds in completely realistic settings.

Write

Here are some notes on two rooms, written down in a writer's notebook and reproduced here just as they came, with no attempt at ordering their randomness.

'A dark room. Two windows, a glass door opening onto the patio. There are two internal doors. A fancy clock ticks a regular tick on the mantelpiece beside three framed photos. Also three small framed sketches of children aged two-and-a-half years and three years old. Dark wood desk with a brown leather top. Brown leather chair on wheels behind the desk. A phone on the desk, a lamp in a Chinese patterned vase. Papers and a notebook; a large calendar; a drawer half open with paper knives, pens, paper clips. Reading glasses with a cord attached left on the desk. A list of soccer fixtures, players and phone numbers on the desk. A telephone statement opened on the desk. Bookshelves full of books and photos. 'Men's Friendship Soccer Tournament Champions over 35, Recreational' clear glass trophy with an emblem of a soccer ball. Telephone directories, family photos of children at different ages. Printer and shredder. A chandelier, wooden floor, with a Chinese rug on the floor. Two small red models of sports cars on a low coffee table. A porche and a corvette.

Books by – James Patterson, Ken Follet, Mario Puzo, Michael Crichton, Sidney Sheldon.

Two more soccer trophies. Computer screen and mouse, printer. Door to outside where a sun lounger sits on the patio. A shelf of books on dreams. Guide to Korea. Another model of a sports car. Pilot's epaulettes. A stack of Automobiles Quarterly magazine.'

As they say on television, who would live in a room like this?

- What sort of person are they?
- Male or female?
- What do they do?

Write a character description of the person who inhabits this room. (250 words)

Write

Notes on a second room:

'Away from the house. Reached by going down some steps and along a path near the swimming pool. Hidden from the house by a dip and behind trees. White room. Cupboards. No radio or TV. Lots of cupboards and drawers, beige carpet. French windows with post-it notes pasted all over them, even the join where the windows open. Doors not used much? Book shelves. Books with catchy, funny titles – Practical Problem Solver, The Joy of Simple Living. Hints, Tips and Smart Advice, Family Circle, Clutter Free Shopping, Caring and Clothing, Cut the Clutter and Stow the Stuff, Clutter's Last Stand. Organising from the Inside Out, The Go of Clutter.

A yoga mat. Bleached wood ceiling with white beams and a skylight in the roof. Light brown wall paper and white wood, simple white. Sea shells on the walls. Simplicity, clear.

A toilet and a washbasin in a small room off the main one. Two chairs, a cosy, oatmeal covered armchair and a brown leather office chair. Nothing with too much colour. Oatmeal and white lattice patterned carpet, French windows with a veranda.'

Again, who would own a room like this?

- What sort of person are they?
- Male or female?
- What do they do?

Write a character description of the person who inhabits this room. (250 words)

Write

To take this further can you link these two characters and these two rooms in some way?

- In what ways are they different? Think about it and make a list. Write them down.
- In what ways are they the same? Think about it and make a list. Write them down.
- How can you connect the two characters in a story?

Write it.

10 TIPS FOR SUCCESS

1 *Settings suggest character.*

2 *Different settings suggest different characters.*

3 *We do not need to be told what a particular setting is if we are given enough clues to set our minds working.*

4 *You do not have to describe a character from outside in minute detail in order to suggest who and what they are.*

5 *A character can be very active, even if they are quite still.*

6 *Description need not be static. If a character is doing something in the setting described, it can come alive for your readers. Animating a character's response to a setting can animate the setting for us.*

7 *Objects can be very evocative of place and character.*

8 *Settings can begin to suggest situations for us; situations can lead to plot lines.*

9 *For character and place, start at the surface and dig.*

10 *People are places and places are people.*

8

Monologue, dialogue and action

In this chapter you will learn:

- about writing monologues
- how dialogue characterizes people
- about the surface world of dialogue
- how to 'novelize' a script.

Key Idea

Dialogue is a very important characterizer. We learn a lot about a person from the way they speak.

Writing monologues for your characters

Dialogue has a huge importance in developing both characters and stories. But before we consider dialogue, which is two or more people speaking, we will look at monologue, which is one person speaking, not to be confused with soliloquy, which is one person's inner thoughts, spoken out loud in plays because the thoughts have to be made audible to the audience. Monologues can be heard by other characters; soliloquies, which are the inner thoughts of a character, cannot.

The British comedy writing team of Laurence Marks and Maurice Gran, writers of *Birds of a Feather, Goodnight Sweetheart, Love Hurts* and *New Statesman*, among others, often write monologues for characters in their sitcoms, particularly in the 'getting to know the character stage' when they are trying to find out about the characters and get the character's individual voice to come out. Writing monologues to get to know your characters is also advice given by James N. Frey in his very good book *How to Write A Damn Good Novel* (1987), the first chapter of which is called 'What it's all About is "Who"' in which he stresses the prime importance of character to stories. Frey suggests writing a character biography in the first person where the character talks about his or her life, not in an encyclopaedic way but in a way that they cover whatever *they* feel is and has been important in their life. He makes the good, practical point that it may be a fragmentary piece with allusions to relationships and work experiences and that it is *not intended for publication*, but will help the author to gain a better understanding of that character from the mouth of the character themselves.

This sort of monologue, where the author is trying to induce the character to speak and make known what the author hopes will be useful, is different from the crafted monologue written to go in a piece or for a performance. Monologues for performance, or monologues which are written to be part of the finished work, such as the *Talking Heads* monologues of Alan Bennett or Molly Bloom's famous monologue in James Joyce's *Ulysses*, need a shape, a form and a purpose. As well as being well written and interesting, that sort of monologue depends on shape and structure, elements which are crucial to stories; the monologues need to be going somewhere, to have a point to them just as a story does, or if part of something, they need to relate to a larger whole.

We are not concerned with crafting the latter type of monologue here. We are going to be concerned with using monologues as a tool to help create and develop strong, believable characters.

One suggestion of Marks and Gran is to write a monologue for each character in your piece as if they were at the doctor's surgery, telling the doctor of their symptoms. Let's use this one.

Write

Take a character from a piece you have written, or take one from one of the pieces you have done from the exercises in this book, or make up a character and write a monologue for them as if they were at the doctor's surgery telling the doctor their symptoms. Just write it and see what comes. (250 words)

What did you learn about the character from the exercise above; anything interesting, surprising or useful? If you did not do it or not a lot happened, try it again with a different character. Just let them talk, don't censor it, see what comes. You are the only one who is going to see it. Surprise yourself.

Write

Write an interior monologue of someone engaged in a tense activity, e.g. a policeman on stake-out, a doctor about to operate, a traffic warden about to swoop on a driver, a shop lifter about to steal something or a store detective about to pounce on a shoplifter.

Go through the stages of:
• anticipation
• event
• outcome (success or failure).

This skeleton will give the monologue a frame and a structure. (250 words)

How did having that small amount of structure change the writing? What difference did you notice between doing this monologue and the one preceding it where the character was speaking to the doctor? Did the structure help or make the writing harder?

How dialogue characterizes people

Dialogue is intimately related to character and characterization. In fact, dialogue is one of the most important tools of characterization.

 ## Key Idea

One of the important elements that will characterize the people in your stories is what they say and how they say it.

 ## Write

Read the lines of dialogue below:

'It's kinda cool cos we get to do like all kinds of stuff.'

'He's like we have to use recycled film because we want it to be so green.'

'And like just really like, we use the edges of what we cut off.'

'And it will be like big pieces stretched out and beyond like this.'

'Last year it wasn't really known at all. I feel like this year I'm only here and it's so weird. I'm looking forward to the next year.'

'It's like we don't really have official work to do.'

'Yeah. There are probably all kinds of rules about that.'

'It's like, I don't know.'

'Did I tell you about this?'

'Yeah.'

'Oh, cool!'

'And we have like this thing that's not like that.'

'It's really cool.'

'It's like, "what is this?"'

'So you know, when I was at school I wasn't thinking like, what will I be doing five years from now. It's like crazy.'

'I feel like we're not connecting. But I need to like get over that. I need to like, take it down a level.'

'I feel like I really don't know.'

- Who are the people speaking?
- What age, background, nationality?
- Where are they?
- Why are they together?
- How do they know each other?
- What do they want in the scene?
- Just what are they talking about?

What other questions do these lines of dialogue raise for you? Take these lines of dialogue and *only these lines of dialogue* and turn them into a scene or the beginning of a story.

- You can write it as a prose piece or a script.
- Do not leave any of the sentences out, use them all.
- You may put them *in any order* you like but do not change them in any other way.
- Add the simple dialogue tags, i.e. 'he said', 'she said' if you wish.
- Add prose links and descriptions between the lines of dialogue.
- Place the characters in a defined setting.

Aim: the main aim is to create a believable scene. Do it now. (500 words)

Were you able to make this exercise work? Which pieces of dialogue presented you with the biggest problems? Were you able to connect them all? Did the characters emerge? What sort of characters did you come up with? What sort of scene and what sort of setting?

See if you can develop it into a larger piece or use it in a piece you are working on.

Key Idea

In your writing you should generally resist the urge to tell us about the characters too much but try to let them emerge through their dialogue and through their interaction with each other.

Write

Read the lines of dialogue below:

'So tell me about Bermondsey. What's it like?'

'There are a lot of antique shops. There's a really good antiques centre. I like it.'

'Where is Bermondsey?

'South London.'

'South London? I thought it was.'

'It's near London Bridge, Tower Bridge.'

'Southwark is the oldest borough outside the city you know.'

'I'm sure it is.'

'It sounds horrible.'

'What?'

'The word, Bermondsey.'

'It does. It used to be pronounced Barmsy.'

'That's nice.'

'It's like balmy isn't it?'

'Yes, that's nicer.'

'There was a lot of damage in the war, very little houses left.'

'So where did you grow up, in a new house, flat, on a council estate?'

'They own it now. It's gentrified now. Why smile? Why did you smile?'

'At the idea of you being gentrified.'

'I didn't say I was gentrified. It is gentrified. Why would I say that? It's nonsense.'

'That's what I thought you said. That's what amused me. That's why I smiled.'

'You shouldn't have smiled. You should have said what a crass, stupid thing to say.'

'Sorry, I smiled again.'

- Who are the people speaking?
- Where are they?
- What age, backgrounds, nationality?
- Why are they together?
- How well do they know each other?

- What do they want in the scene?
- What is going on here?

Take these lines of dialogue and *only these lines of dialogue* and turn them into a scene or the beginning of a story.

- Use them all.
- Keep them *in this order*.
- Add the simple dialogue tags, i.e. 'he said,' 'she said' if you wish.
- Do not leave any of the sentences out, use them all.
- Do not change them in any way.
- Place the characters in a clear setting.

Aim: once again the main aim is to create a believable scene. Resist the urge to tell us about the characters too much, try to let the characters emerge through this dialogue and through their interaction. Do not worry about who the people are before you write, just let the characters emerge from what they say. Do it now. (500 words)

Did the characters emerge? What sort of characters did you come up with? Were they quite different to the characters you came up with in the previous exercise or were they similar? What difference did it make keeping the dialogue in the order in which it was written? Did you prefer the randomness of being able to change the order or did it help to keep the lines as they were? Think about these questions and about your answers.

Write

Can you write the next scene of the story you have started above? Try it; do it now. (500 words)

The surface world of dialogue

Dialogue in scripts is a special case. There are always many 'things unsaid', for want of a better way of putting it, in and around the dialogue in a script. One of the big problems that novelists and story writers have in writing scripts is trying to write 'the things you don't actually write'. Novelists and story writers want to write it all in. The scriptwriter's task is to know it all but to leave 90% of it out (and rely on other people, such as the director and actors, to look for it and have the skills to find it).

Key Idea

The particular task of anyone creating characters in a script is to know what to put in and, as importantly, what to leave out.

Scripts are written with both what is on the paper and what is not on the paper. In a script, the words on the page are only a proportion of the entire piece and actors and directors spend their time in rehearsal trying to find and mine the rest of the work which is somehow suggested by the white paper, the blank spaces which point to what is not written down but which is nevertheless there. It is the writer who puts them there. It is like writing in invisible ink.

WRITING IN INVISIBLE INK

To create characters in a script, we need to put down what the character does and says, not only to others but also to themselves. We need to give them actions to perform and have consequences flow from them doing what they do, which in turn affect and alter the picture that we have of them. We need to see characters performing actions that work upon others, and on themselves, saying lines that others react to and which they themselves react to. This is how the character will grow for us.

Key Idea

Action and reaction is one of the mainsprings of character creation and also of plotting. This action and reaction, this back and forwarding is what pushes the story along. It is where character and plot work together.

Case Study: The Cherry Orchard

In his last play, *The Cherry Orchard*, first staged in Moscow in 1904, Chekhov shows he is a writer capable of creating heartbreaking scenes of love. There is a famous scene, late in the play, between two characters Varya and Lopakhin. They have been 'intended' for each other for a long time in theirs and many people's minds and towards the end of the play find themselves left alone together just so that Lopakhin can propose to Varya. Unfortunately, this being Chekhov, they fail and the moment passes in a stream of superficial inconsequential remarks. They talk about the weather and other banalities until finally Lopakhin is called away by a workman. He rushes out in relief, never proposes and the moment is gone. It is tragically poignant. The two characters, who might have gone one way in life, together, both head off to their different futures having failed to capitalize on the big moment.

If you read what Chekhov has written on the page in *The Cherry Orchard*, the surface of the script is quite ordinary and inconsequential. Just reading the surface, you could miss what is really going on inside the characters and in the story; the encounter would go for nothing. The relationship between the surface and what is hidden needs to be fully appreciated and understood. Chekhov understood it. He understood that what he was writing on the page was the means by which he 'wrote' what was, as it were, *beneath* the page, what was *hidden*, what was *suggested*, what was *invisible*, what was *inner*. In his stage plays, Chekhov was a master at finding outer ways to reveal the inner life of his characters.

In the scene outlined above, Chekhov has written the most ordinary exchanges for the characters on the surface, while beneath the surface there is so much more going on in emotional and story terms. This is a momentous meeting that will change and seal these two characters' lives and it is as if the two characters are standing on an ice floe and are afraid to move. The ice is their ordinary realm and they are not able to plunge beneath it into the currents moving below. They stay up on the ice where they are safe, where they and their world are known and do not risk the swift icy currents of the emotional waters beneath. Who can blame them? Which of us would want to plunge into water that could sweep us away?

In plot terms the action builds to a climax in the scene but the climax does not happen, rather it falls away. Much in life happens like this. Opportunities pass and close over before we are really aware they were opportunities. We always think there will be another time and there rarely is. A Hollywood film would not be able to put up with such an ending. This would have to be followed by a final scene where the two intended met once again, where this time the climax did happen. But not for Chekhov; he was writing truth. Neither of the characters voiced their feelings. For them and for Chekhov this was the right course to take.

At this moment in his play, there is a 'surface world', a safe world, a known world. Everyday life, what has become the norm, is not punctured; it remains intact and the two characters remain clinging to it. Who knows what would have happened to the characters had they taken the plunge and declared their love for each other in climactic fashion? But it is as if they were too cautious, too fearful of puncturing the surface world in which they lived. Chekhov understood that life is more like this than it is like a movie version of it.

Write

Think of two characters who both want something. For example, to be together, to go on holiday together, to play in the same sports team together, or in the same theatre production. Write a scene in which the two characters will not admit this and talk about anything else but this. (250 words)

Case Study: Uncle Vanya

This same need for a character to puncture the surface reality of their world comes in another, earlier Chekhov play, *Uncle Vanya*, which premiered in Moscow in 1899. This time it occurs a little earlier in the play, in Act 3, but it too is a highly significant and emotionally charged moment which pushes the play on towards its end. Love, or infatuation, has been building between several of the characters before the play starts and throughout the play, and this time the surface world *is* punctured.

Vanya is managing the country estate for his brother-in-law, the husband of Vanya's now dead sister, a retired university professor named Aleksandr Vladimirovich Serebryakov. The professor has a young and beautiful 27-year-old wife, Elena Andreyevna Serebryako. They have come to the country to stay and Vanya has become infatuated with Elena, following her around and hopelessly in love. Vanya's niece, Sonya loves the local doctor, Astrov, but she has never spoken to him of it. Sonya likes the doctor to visit; she likes to see him, to watch him and to hear his voice. Sonya has come to settle for this but in Act 3, when she confesses this to Elena, Elena suggests that Sonya needs to know where she stands and she takes it upon herself to speak to Astrov and to ascertain the doctor's feelings for Sonya. Sonya is hesitant; is it better to know and risk having her dream shattered, or to stay in the dreamland of possibility? Elena says she must know and if he does not love her, then it is for the best that the doctor is told he should not come there anymore. Elena sends for him and waits for the doctor to come to her.

Again, as in all of Chekhov's plays, there is a surface world and a world moving beneath that surface. In the scene above, on the surface Elena is planning to draw out Astrov's feelings for Sonya, but beneath the surface, she too secretly finds him attractive. We, the audience, have become aware by now that the doctor also finds Elena attractive. We also, in the audience, know that he is not in love with Sonya, so the entire scene is fraught with dramatic possibility, tension and irony.

Dramatic irony is a staple dramatic device where the audience is in possession of information that the characters are not aware of. It also is very much a part of the surface/reality relationship. In this scene, we watch the characters move around each other in ways that they are not able to discern themselves. We see their conscious behaviour and their unconscious desires in a sort of dance or on a series of shifting planes. We see them express conscious, surface reasons while also witnessing the playing out of their unconscious drives and needs. In scripts, the writer is writing both these elements at the same time, the visible and the invisible. Chekhov handles them with mastery. Actors need to handle these two 'planes of emotion' as well in performance.

The surface elements of the scene in *Uncle Vanya* described above are very ordinary; the characters are in a room and they talk, but at the same time the other forces, the emotional forces, move with force and passion beneath them, so Chekhov shows us the encounter taking place on two levels at the same time. With the true drama of theatre we are able watch this as the two characters, Elena and Astrov, meet in a surface reality *and* simultaneously in a reality much deeper.

Astrov and Elena have not been alone together before but it is a moment they have been moving towards, a moment that has been inevitable in the play. In the social world at this time – structured and ordered as it is so that women do not spend time alone with men without being chaperoned – it is a dangerous moment. The doctor's surface story is that he is interested in the environment. His hidden story is that he is interested in Elena. Elena's surface story is that she would like to ask him about his feelings for Sonya, for Sonya's sake. Her hidden story is that she would like to ask Astrov about his feelings for her, for her own sake. The two characters live in a mundane surface world with a more desperate world of love and need and desire, a world needing love beneath it and Chekhov's genius is to present these two realities simultaneously to us in the same moment up on the stage so that we can see and understand the relationship between the two levels.

Peter Nichols in his 1981 play *Passion Play* made the invisible visible for us, with two characters in a marriage that is falling apart actually on stage with their alter egos, played by other actors, who speak the truths that the characters in the surface world will not and do not say. This is perhaps the sort of thing that a realistic medium like film might have to do, if it did it at all, in a rather mechanical way with something like a split screen.

In the theatre, Astrov and Elena come together under the pretext of the doctor showing her his maps of the area, maps which highlight the environmental changes that have been taking place over the years, something about which he is quite passionate. For some long moments they stay on the surface of this surface world. As in the scene discussed from *The Cherry Orchard*, on the page, the surface of words that Chekhov gives us, this encounter reads deadly dull. Astrov goes through a series of maps and statistics and talks in a very long monologue about the reducing flora and fauna shown in different colours on his maps. Was ever a woman wooed in this manner? Elena tries to show interest in his monologue but her mind is not on it at all, and nor is his. He is glad to be alone with her and talks nervously to fill the awkward silence which, if he did not, would allow the hidden truths and desires to come tumbling out. He is also no doubt seeking to impress her, showing her all of his hard work in documenting the depletion of the area's natural resources and how much it concerns him. It is a fine example of how a surface reality, which appears calm and mundane, is charged with passion and a danger which slides like sharks beneath.

Elena listens to him for a long time but she has her own agenda. She knows she has to bring the discussion round to Sonya. She must ask him if he loves Sonya. If yes, then he must declare it. If no, then he must go away, never return and break Sonya's heart. It is a chore she does not relish, not least because she is also interested in the doctor and anxious in case his answer is yes. In asking him to declare his feelings for Sonya, she will really be asking him to declare his feelings for her. And we know that he wants to declare his feelings for her too. In their inner selves they probably both know it and this is what has been drawing them together. For as long as possible they try to keep their inner selves apart, staying in the surface world, the outer world of maps and flora and fauna and the changing environment, while the hidden world of their hidden selves is drawing them closer and closer together.

A theatre production filmed at Chichester in 1963 had Laurence Olivier and Rosemary Harris circling each other, coming together then moving away. They almost touched hands; they didn't. The outer physical behaviour mimicked the inner world of doubt and emotion. This scene was a most perfect dance of the two worlds, a dance of opposing partnership.

Eventually Elena asks the questions about Sonya and Astrov confesses that he does not love Sonya. Elena says he must not come there again and expresses relief that her disagreeable duty is over. But now the unspoken has been spoken. Love has been mentioned, or desire at any rate. There is a breach. The air between them has been punctured and the two worlds, the inner and the outer, the surface and the hidden, are in danger of bursting and flowing into one another, causing chaos. And where the hidden feelings do not come out in the scene between Varya and Lopakhin in *The Cherry Orchard*, presumably because they are not actually that strong, here they are too strong to be denied and they do come out. The moment does not close over mundanely. Now the inner world has been made outer, chaos ensues; it cannot be held back.

The doctor now challenges Elena. If he goes and never comes back because of Sonya, then he will be faced with the prospect of not seeing her, Elena, again. He asks why she had to ask him now, at this time; why she had to take it on herself, and answers that it was because she is interested in him. He knows that she wants him and he tells her that he is hers. She feigns embarrassment. He says she must come and eat him up, devour him. Openly stating what was unspoken, bringing into the light what was hidden now threatens her in a fundamental way. She can no longer deny her hidden feelings; she can no longer live in a world of pretence. She is married to a much older man who is irritable and bothered by pains. Now interest in another man has been spoken. She must embrace it or run away.

The doctor, an experienced man of the world, suggests they quickly make arrangements before someone else interrupts them. He immediately raises practical questions such as where shall they meet. He embraces and kisses her, she struggles and at this moment the totally lovesick Vanya enters with a bunch of flowers for her. Once he sees Elena and Astrov in each other's arms, *his* dreams of love are shattered. He bumbles out, crushed. The tears and laughter, with Chekhov, as they do in life, come at the same time.

This play is not just a comedy of manners. It is not just the surface world of convention and decorum that has been breached, allowing out all sorts of hidden passions. For Elena, the inner world of hidden emotions now threaten to engulf her entirely. Fearing that she will be swept away, she rushes off declaring that she has to leave the house at once. She pleads with her husband to take her away.

She is either an honourable woman who does not want to be prey to these emotions or a fearful woman who fears the consequences of letting go.

Chekhov is a master at handing the relationship between the inner and the outer worlds, the surface and the hidden, the visible and the invisible. He is a master of the tragi-comedy of it all. He gives us a surface reality that allows us to access what lies beneath. We can only see what is beneath because of the carefully constructed artifice of language and silences: movement and stillness, speech and silence. The mastery that you are moving towards as a writer is to become able to write what you can't see as well as what you can see, to create the invisible world beneath the character surface as well as the visible.

 ## Key Idea

At a certain level in our writing, we get to the stage where we reach for the invisible by creating what is visible. We write one thing in order to write something else. We attempt to hit a target by not aiming at it. We put marks on paper that are marks on paper but which we hope will stand for or let us look through to something else. That is why writing is not written in stone, but rather it is written in water or in air.

Great art mirrors, mimics or creates equivalents to life. Just as we cannot sustain unruly passions forever in our lives and need to settle in the plain and the ordinary, so it is with art. The inner life is contained by the outer life and flows in and through the outer life. The inner life can only be made known through the outer life. In stories the inner lives of the characters, the inner truths of the story can only be made manifest through the outer presentation. In Chekhov's plays, it is safe for characters to stay in the outer world, the ordinary world of maps and samovars and chitchat but the consequences of neglecting the inner life can be very serious; it is always there, threatening to pour out and engulf the characters. But when it does pour out, as it does in *Uncle Vanya*, there has to be a resolution. After Elena and her husband leave, Vanya and Sonya settle back into the ordinary world in which the play started, doing the accounts, fulfilling the ordinary obligations which make up the boring drudgery of life. Chekhov knows that the mundane is where we live.

HOW DO YOU WRITE WHAT IS HIDDEN?

It is not easy to suggest exercises by which you might practise writing what you are not actually writing. To do this is highly sophisticated; it is writing that is at the top of the tree. It is something you need to develop yourself over time and the only way to develop it is through writing and writing. The more you write, the more your writing should inevitably deepen. But, perhaps the unseen can at least be approached through metaphor.

To write what is hidden you need to understand something about hitting a target by aiming at something else; something about metaphor. To write what is hidden, you need to write a scene in a story or a film where the purpose is not to show what is beneath the surface, e.g. duplicity or treachery, but the surface of which stands for something else. There is a scene in *Anna Karenina* where Count Vronsky pets and strokes and whispers to his excitable horse Frou Frou in a way incredibly suggestive of the way he must be intimate with Anna. It is a lovely piece of writing in which the author is writing one thing while telling us about something else.

Some scenes in some films work on more than one plane by using metaphor. The game of chess is used to suggest sex in *The Thomas Crown Affair* where the two stars, Steve McQueen and Faye Dunaway, play a game of chess in a flirtatious manner. They look at each other, lick their lips and caress the chess pieces like body parts and the camera and lighting and music all add to the colouring. Food is used to suggest a very similar thing in another well-known film scene, this time from the 1963 comedy film adaptation of Henry Fielding's novel *Tom Jones*. In a scene without dialogue, Tom and Mrs Waters sit opposite each other in the dining room of the Upton Inn, consuming a large meal with again much lustful looking and finger and lip licking. Eating is used for a different purpose in the film *Angel Heart*. Robert de Niro playing a character called Louis Cyphre, which is a not very subtle name for Lucifer, sits opposite the Micky Rourke character eating hard-boiled eggs in a way suggestive of the devil consuming human souls. We know that though the Rourke character might struggle and deny, the devil will also eat his soul.

Write

Write a scene with two people in it, performing an activity, such as playing a game or dancing, which on the surface means one thing for both participants but which has another meaning for them beneath the surface. They are doing one thing but thinking quite another. (200 words)

Did you find the above exercise easy or hard? What did you learn from it?

Whether you found it easy or hard, do it again using a different activity. See what happens this time.

How to 'novelize' a script

Your task in the exercise below will be to find what is left unsaid in a script and decide what you want to realize as a prose piece.

Read the dialogue that follows.

A busy café. MIKE and SHAZZA sitting at a table.

MIKE	Shazza, this can go no further.
SHAZZA	What?
MIKE	You know what.
SHAZZA	Do you think I fancy you?
MIKE	I'm not arrogant enough to think that, but there's something I wanted to say. I'm married.
SHAZZA	I know you're married. You're warning me off and I haven't said anything.
MIKE	I wanted to make explicit what seemed to be implicit.
SHAZZA	I haven't said anything. You started this conversation.
MIKE	Well, all right, if I misread the situation then I apologize. Forget I said anything.
SHAZZA	You're yawning.
MIKE	I was about to cough and I didn't want to cough all over you. (Pause)
SHAZZA	I went for a drink with Jim and he sat there. He's got a wife and three kids at home and he was flirting with me.
MIKE	You're saying Mr Coombes wanted you?

SHAZZA	He wanted me. I wouldn't have liked to have been his wife.
MIKE	What would you have done?
SHAZZA	Killed him.
MIKE	I can imagine. You didn't want him?
SHAZZA	I can want people until they're obtainable…
MIKE	Have you ever done that? Had an affair with a married man?
SHAZZA	No. I wouldn't make a good mistress. I wouldn't play by the rules.
MIKE	No, you'd be dangerous.
SHAZZA	Am I dangerous?
MIKE	Very.
SHAZZA	I'd probably pull him in by being all sweet and nice and then hate him.
MIKE	Hate him? Why would you hate him?
SHAZZA	*(Quietly, as if she's revealed too much of herself.)* I wouldn't hate him.
MIKE	Well I can tell you aren't trying to pull me in. Because you aren't being sweet and nice to me.
SHAZZA	Aren't I? I thought I was.
MIKE	Well you're falling short, the mask keeps slipping.
SHAZZA	You don't like me very much do you? What would you do if I tried to kiss you? What if I made a pass at you?
MIKE	I'd have to refuse it.
SHAZZA	You wouldn't be able to resist me. Men are like that. They like it. They like sex. What if I wouldn't let you say no?
MIKE	Women don't behave that way.
SHAZZA	Oh you live in the past. I would. I behave that way.
MIKE	Then I'd fight you off. It wouldn't be hard.
SHAZZA	Would you? Would you really? What if I said I wanted to shag you? What would you do?
MIKE	You'd have to say it.
SHAZZA	I really want to shag you.
MIKE	Well you can't.
SHAZZA	I hate you. I don't like you. You don't like me, do you? Why agree to meet me?
MIKE	Why not?
SHAZZA	Don't cop out of my question.
MIKE	I wanted to. I like you. I wanted to see if we could develop our friendship; keep our friendship without going any further.

SHAZZA	You must be a bit tempted. You could have great sex with me.
MIKE	I'm going home.
SHAZZA	You're a flirt, just a flirt. You flirt. You should stop flirting so much.
MIKE	Okay, so I flirt, everyone flirts, but does it need to go any further than that?
SHAZZA	Shall I tell you the truth? I really fancy you. I want to make wild passionate love to you.
MIKE	No you don't.
SHAZZA	I do. No one would know.
MIKE	I would know. I hope.
SHAZZA	Kiss me.
MIKE	No.
SHAZZA	Hold me. Kiss me. Look, I know you're married. Come for a drink with me.
MIKE	I have to go.
SHAZZA	You don't want to. Stop being so demure.
MIKE	I do want to. I want to go.
SHAZZA	Will you see me again?
MIKE	I don't mind seeing you again.
SHAZZA	See, if you really wanted to end it, you'd say you didn't want to see me. Kiss me.
MIKE	I can't.
SHAZZA	Go then. I hate you.
	(Mike stands up.)
MIKE	Goodbye.
SHAZZA	Goodbye. That's not a very good way to say goodbye. You're not very nice. You're horrible. I hate you.
	(Mike leaves the café. Outside he takes out his mobile phone and dials.)
MIKE	Headmaster? I need to speak to you, urgently. Today, now if possible.

Do you agree that there is a lot in this scene which is not on the page? If not, read it again. This piece should raise questions for you:

- Who are the people speaking?
- Where are they?
- Why are they together?
- What is their relationship?
- What is going on in the scene beneath the words?
- Who wants what in the scene?
- Who drives the scene? (Who is in charge?)

- Who has the power in the scene?
- Does it shift at all?

Write

Take these lines of dialogue and *only these lines of dialogue*, keeping the piece in the order in which it is written, and fully 'novelize' it.

- Use all the lines.
- Keep them in this order.
- Do not change them in any way but add dialogue tags, i.e. 'he said', 'she said'.
- Make full use of prose links and descriptions.
- Use interior thought.
- Place the characters in a fully realized setting.

Aim: the main aim is to create a believable scene but this time to learn how to mine a script and bring the invisible into the visible world. You will also characterize two characters while practising the relationship between dialogue and prose. (1000 words)

How did you go? Did the characters emerge? What sort of characters did you come up with?

Think about these questions and about your answers.

1 *Writing monologues is a good way of letting characters tell you about themselves.*

2 *When your character speaks, listen to them.*

3 *Action and dialogue are crucial for revealing a character's inner life.*

4 *How a character acts and reacts to situations and setbacks is vital to creating life and energy in a character.*

5 *Character and plot are intimately connected.*

6 *When events break through the surface reality of a character or a story, that world can never be the same: chaos ensues.*

7 *Mastery of character is the ability to create what you are not creating; to write what you are not writing.*

8 *Writing a prose story and writing a script are quite different.*

9 *Writing is not only about what is said but also what is unsaid.*

10 *Writers need to know what to put in and what to leave out.*

9

Character and viewpoint

In this chapter you will learn:
- about viewpoint characters
- how to find the right voice
- that narrators are not always as they seem.

Who will tell the story?

The choice of viewpoint character is one of the most important decisions you will take as a writer. 'Viewpoint character' means the character whose head you will get inside as the writer and therefore through whose eyes your readers and viewers will experience the story. Whatever you decide will have a huge influence on your character and how the story is expressed and experienced.

There are several modes you can take to tell a prose story but the most frequently used and therefore the most relevant to look at are *first person* and *third person*.

FIRST PERSON

This story is told by a narrator who is *also a character in the story*. This form is easily identified because the author writes using 'I'. 'I did this. I did that. I wanted this. I wanted that.' Many acclaimed novels have been written from this viewpoint: *Catcher in the Rye* by J. D. Salinger, Mark Twain's *Adventures of Huckleberry Finn*, and *The Sun Also Rises* by Ernest Hemmingway are three very well-known first person stories. Alice Sebold's 2002 novel, *The Lovely Bones*, had a lot of success in many ways because of the choice of narrator made by the author. The narrator was a teenage girl who had been raped, murdered and dismembered, narrating her story from heaven. A murdered narrator had famously been used before, of course, that of the dead body floating in the pool in Billy Wilder's much lauded movie *Sunset Boulevard*.

The first person narrator may not always be liked or laudable, but their 'voices', the sound their words make, the resonance they strike in the readers, is a crucial part of the story fabric. We get to know the character well and are drawn into the story and its world through the voice of the first person viewpoint character. The narrator may be intelligent or dim, rich or poor, articulate or inarticulate, victim or aggressor, alive or dead, but what they have to say and the way they tell it are a very important part of the involvement, enjoyment and meaning of a first person story. It is as if a real person were speaking directly to us and telling us their tale.

THIRD PERSON

This story is told by the author using 'he', 'she', 'it', or 'they' and never by using 'I' or 'we'. For example, 'He went down the road and bought a newspaper from the sweet shop. The woman behind the counter spoke to him. As he left he spoke to her dog which was tied up outside the shop. It was wet and unhappy and it was very hungry.'

The voice telling the story is not a character in the story but an observer. This does not mean any necessary loss of immediacy or that we are not drawn into the story. On the contrary, third person narratives can be both immediate and involving. The majority of novels published are written in third person, not first person.

But third person is not so clear-cut as first person. There are two forms of third person viewpoint that you need to know and master: third person limited, and third person omniscient or omnipotent.

Third person omniscient or omnipotent viewpoint

This was the most commonly used form of narration up to and well through the nineteenth century. Classic novelists such as Jane Austen, Charles Dickens, George Eliot, Henry James, Leo Tolstoy and Anthony Trollope all wrote their novels in the voice of the third person omniscient narrator. This mode is of course written in the third person, i.e. using 'he', 'she', 'it', or 'they', but the clue to this voice is in the description 'omniscient' or 'omnipotent'. The voice in this form is an all-knowing, all-powerful, 'godlike' voice that sees into all the characters' heads, into all the places in the story and moves effortlessly from character to character and from place to place.

Style, and again 'voice', is a crucial element of writing in this form. The classic writers using this form all developed distinctive 'voices'. The tone of a Jane Austen novel is very much an essential part of the story she tells, equally so for Trollope, Dickens and all the others. A large part of the enjoyment of their stories is enjoyment of their voices; of the way they use language to present worlds that are rich and full of characters and situations. This storytelling voice is characterized by both closeness and distance. Both Austen and Trollope can present characters to us in a way that, with deft touches of insight or irony, at the same time undercuts them. A character like Mr Collins in *Pride and Prejudice* might see himself in one light, while other characters in the story see him quite differently, but it is the all-knowing voice of the author, through the way she both presents and comments on him ironically, that we are able to see him in this other, amusing light. The same is true with the character of the Reverend Slope in *Barchester Towers*. When Trollope tells us that Slope had at some point in his life added an 'e' to his name 'for the sake of euphony', we are able to laugh with the author at the former Reverend Slop. We learn a good deal about these characters while also enjoying the authors' wicked humour at their expense.

Characteristic of the omniscient viewpoint is that the author has both closeness to the characters (they tell us what they are thinking and feeling) and distance from them (they comment on them). Characters in this sort of story are held at a distance by the author because it is the author and their strong voice that we are listening to. We do not get inside the characters' heads and hearts, except by invitation and direction of the author. The author conducts the story and directs our responses, both emotional and intellectual. With the great authors a large part of the enjoyment of the tales they tell is the way they tell them, how they guide us.

But as confidence in authority in all its forms waned, and as movies and television developed and affected the way audiences experienced narrative, the third person omniscient narrator became much less used in the twentieth century and remains less favoured in the twenty-first century. It is still possible to write novels in this mode but the most used form today is third person *limited*.

Third person limited

This, as a phrase, explains itself. Writing in this form is again written in the third person, i.e. using 'he', 'she', 'it', or 'they', but it is 'limited' not 'omniscient'. It is 'limited' in that it is *not* all-seeing; it is not godlike. It is human and it takes a limited perspective on characters and events. Instead of the wide overarching view encompassing as many characters as it wishes of the omniscient viewpoint, the limited viewpoint is closer to first person in that the author confines themselves to one head, one brain and one pair of eyes, at least *at a time*.

Finding the right voice

To see the difference between the two third person viewpoints, let's look at some examples.

THIRD PERSON OMNISCIENT OR OMNIPOTENT VIEWPOINT

He went down the same road where 2000 years earlier a Roman legion had marched over the bones of his Celtic ancestors and bought a newspaper from a shop on which a Roman villa had once stood. The woman who spoke to him took his money, deeply hating him all the while. Out of sight behind the dirty window she cursed him as he bent and consoled her hungry, wet and unhappy dog that lay looking up hopefully into the only pair of human eyes that had ever been kind to it.

This narrator knows everything: about the road's Roman past, the woman's present hatred of the man and the unhappy state of the dog. We are not solely confined to the thoughts and perceptions of the woman, the man, or the dog. We are in the hands of a narrator who does not feel solely confined to one character or to one time frame either. This narrator is capable of telling us about the characters and the situations in which they find themselves, both in history and at the same time in the here and now.

The difference between omniscient and limited viewpoint can be shown if we rewrite the same scene in third person limited. Unlike the omniscient, we *will* be limited to the man, the woman *or* the dog.

THIRD PERSON LIMITED VIEWPOINT

He went down the same road where 2000 years earlier a Roman legion had marched over the bones of his Celtic ancestors and bought a newspaper from a shop on which a Roman villa had once stood. The woman who spoke to him took his money while giving him a funny look. He thought he glimpsed her trying to stay out of sight behind her dirty window as he bent and consoled her hungry, wet and unhappy dog.

Our viewpoint here is the man. We are with him as we experience the scene. He knows about the Roman past and the villa and his Celtic ancestors, so maybe he is an archaeologist. But he does not know about the woman's hatred for him, though he senses something 'funny' in the look she gives him. If we wanted to give a different picture, we could write 'angry look' or 'irritated look' or something else. But whatever we chose to write, it would be *his* perception of it and not necessarily what she was feeling. He also does not see inside the dog's head. He is limited to what he sees or senses and what he makes of it. He definitely thinks he sees her trying to stay out of sight while he pats her unhappy dog. And he judges that the dog is hungry and unhappy – that is an assessment that he makes from its body language – and possibly a judgement that is critical of the woman too. But all of his perceptions are limited. They have boundaries and the limits are what he can see, hear, touch, taste and smell; what he can apprehend or otherwise reason out.

Let's look at the same scene limited to the woman's point of view.

She watched him come down the same road where 2000 years earlier a Roman legion had marched over the bones of his Celtic ancestors and come into her shop on which a Roman villa had once stood. She took his money, deeply hating him all the while. Keeping out of sight behind the dirty window she cursed him as he bent and said something to her dog.

In this version we are very strongly inside her head and her hatred comes over powerfully. *She* sees him coming down the road. *She* knows about the Roman past this time, so in this version *she* has the archaeological knowledge. But here you somehow get a sense of her taking pleasure in thinking that the legions had marched over the bones of his ancestors. She also takes his money, deeply hating him all the while. We can feel that hatred as she takes the money, possibly with a smile; after all, money is money. Of *his* feelings or reaction we know nothing, because she does not know or try and guess them. Maybe her own feelings are so strong that she does not care what he is feeling. When he goes outside she watches him pet her dog; not her 'hungry, wet and unhappy dog' because she does not see the dog that way. To see it that way would be making a judgement on herself. The 'hungry, wet and unhappy dog' is the judgement of someone else's eyes. To her the dog is just her dog. It is her possession. Somehow you can feel her rage burning through the glass that he dares to pet *her* dog.

Interestingly, if she did judge herself from *outside*, that would be a viewpoint slip, an inconsistency in viewpoint. We will look at this issue in a moment, but from this brief exercise you can see how subtle, complex and interesting viewpoint can be. The viewpoint character in your story is the one through whose eyes the reader will experience what happens, and in the third person limited viewpoint, the limited viewpoint character is human not godlike; there are limits to what they can therefore see and hear; they do not hear everything. The limited narrator may partially know themselves and have some knowledge of some people, but they do not know everything about all people at all times. They can only tell us about what they see or know or believe or have found out, they cannot, for instance, tell us what another character is thinking, as can the omniscient author.

The limited viewpoint character can guess at what another character is thinking, or surmise it from their behavior, but they are limited to the evidence they can come up with – the thoughts and perceptions of their own heads – and are not privy to the private cogitations of others.

Hence the man in our example sees the woman give him a 'funny look,' but without knowing that she deeply hates him. You can also see how the narrative can alter or be altered by changing your viewpoint character. The same scene can appear different depending on through whose eyes it is seen. Our example shows clearly the differences in third person limited and third person omniscient in this regard. In the limited version, we are either in the man's head or we are in the woman's head. We are not in both, as we are in the omniscient method.

CHANGING VIEWPOINT AND VIEWPOINT SLIPS

If you are to make the characters and the narrative convincing in a third person limited viewpoint piece, you must not slip in viewpoint. You must not move from one head to another without signalling it clearly to the reader. However, slips can occur in other ways, for example, as we just mentioned, allowing the woman to judge herself from outside herself, with the eyes of another. You could also slip by having a character tell us something they could not possibly have seen or witnessed or known about. Slipping in viewpoint can seriously affect the credibility of your story, so you must be consistent. But slipping in viewpoint and *changing* viewpoint are not the same thing.

It is not the case that you can and must only have one viewpoint character throughout a whole story, though there are often very good reasons for doing just that – certainly, when you are starting out, it is not a bad decision to limit the number of viewpoint characters. Whereas omniscient authors move freely between the thoughts of one character and another and do this in the middle of scenes, and in the middle of sentences, writers using the limited mode need to signal a change of viewpoint character carefully, ideally changing from one character to another at the start of different chapters, or different scenes, never in the middle of scenes and never in the middle of a sentence. To do that is most confusing for the reader.

Key Idea

If you are in one head, stay there. When you vacate that head, to go to another, help the reader by making it clear when you leave and where you go.

Let's look at the same scene we have already looked at and try to see what happens if we slip between the woman and the man's point of view while writing in third person limited viewpoint.

> *She watched him come down the same road where 2000 years earlier a Roman legion had marched over the bones of his Celtic ancestors and enter her shop on which a Roman villa had once stood. She took his money, deeply hating him all the while. He*

thought she gave him a funny look and also thought he glimpsed
her trying to stay out of sight behind her dirty window as he
bent and consoled her hungry, wet and unhappy dog that she left
all day tied up outside and who now lay looking into the only
human eyes who were ever kind to it.

We start with her watching him come down the road and we end up in the dog's head! The viewpoint is set up clearly at the start; we are with *her*, so where does this switch take place? Read it over to be sure. Yes, there are two.

The first one comes after the word 'while'. 'He thought she gave him a funny look' is *his* thought about their meeting. Maybe you think this viewpoint switch works. It does change in a clear place; one moment we are with the woman, the next we are with the man, but there is a second switch: a switch from inside the man to inside the dog. What do you think of this viewpoint switch? Read the last sentence again to make sure you understand where the switch takes place and then decide what you think of it.

The problem here is that the piece begins in third person limited – and third person limited is not third person omniscient. In third person limited the writer agrees a contract with the reader to tell a story, or at least a part of it, from a particular point of view. It is a contract entered into by both parties. The contract states that the writer will construct the narrative from a particular point of view and will not deviate from that. If he wants to change, he will make the change clear and firm. Both parties know the contract and generally abide by it. If the contract is broken, then consequences ensue. Rather than break the contract by slipping from one head into another, from man to dog like this, it is much more helpful to the reader if you change viewpoint character at the end of a scene or at least a paragraph and not mid-scene or mid-paragraph or mid-sentence.

Let's try it again:

He went down the same road where 2000 years earlier a Roman
legion had marched over the bones of his Celtic ancestors and
bought a newspaper from a shop on which a Roman villa had
once stood. The woman who spoke to him took his money,
deeply hating him all the while. Out of sight behind the dirty
window she cursed him as he bent and said something to her dog.

We appear to be in the man's head at the start but through this paragraph we go from his head to hers and we do it mid-sentence.

We are with him up until the word 'money'. He does not think the thought that follows, *'deeply hating him all the while.'* She does;

that is where the transfer takes place. She has become our viewpoint character. But do we stay with her? Where are we as she watches him with her dog *'out of sight'* outside the shop? Are we with her viewpoint or back with his? She cannot be out of sight to herself, so is it his? But then how can he know she is there if she is out of sight? Does it mean she is out of *his* sight behind the window? Maybe it is just carelessly written but you can see how dangerously slippery viewpoint can become if it is not handled precisely.

Again, you might want to argue that writing it like this is all right; we worked it out. But can you imagine how potentially wearing and confusing this would be in a long piece if the writing continually slid from one character to another and you had to check back to see which character you were with? Writing in third person limited viewpoint, your choice of viewpoint character is an important decision to take; at any point in the story it is an absolute position to take up and one you must be consistent with *until you change it*. And if you are to change, it must be deliberate and clear. You must not slide in and out of viewpoint characters carelessly. To do so runs the risk of destabilizing your writing and your reader, who will not know where you are or they are.

In summary, you can bring a lot of interest to a story through changing viewpoints from one character to another, but you must not make it confusing for the reader to follow. In third person limited, if you do change from one character to another in your story, you need to signal the change clearly so that the reader knows through whose eyes they are now witnessing the events, because each time they change, the new character is also limited to what they observe, know, believe or surmise. But changing viewpoint can add new dimensions to a piece of writing. If handled interestingly and well, viewpoint can bring out a range of different features of a character and of a story.

Key Idea

Choosing the right viewpoint character for an entire novel, or for part of a story, can be a crucial decision to make. It can impact on character and on story. And once you tell a reader that you are telling the story through the eyes of a particular character, then that is the viewpoint you must stick with, *until you signal a deliberate change*. If you do not make clear any change, you risk destabilizing the reader and leaving them not knowing where they are.

WHICH NARRATIVE MODE?

Let's look again at the opening paragraph of the piece we discussed on setting in an earlier chapter.

> *He walked up the steps cutting the steep lawns, past signs to the library and the Schoenberg music block till he found the spot, the walkway between the library and another building. The walkway was lined with cypress trees and cast iron street lamps with glass bulbs on top to illuminate the path at night. They were unlit now except by the quiet glow which came from the daylight resting in them. He wondered what light they gave at night, particularly how dark and safe this walkway was. He walked up and down the walkway twice, looking very carefully from side to side and behind each bench and cypress tree then stopped and sat on a flat stone bench next to some scattered peanut shells. They lay broken open by something human or something rodent like, a squirrel or a rat.*

What narrative mode is this written in?

- First person?
- Third person omniscient?
- Third person limited?

You should be able to tell that this is written in third person limited viewpoint. We are limited to the thoughts and perceptions of the central character and this stays consistently so throughout the piece. But in order to further examine viewpoint and to see what effects it can have, let's try rewriting this in the **first person mode:**

> *I walked up the steps cutting the steep lawns, past signs to the library and the Schoenberg music block till I found the spot, the walkway between the library and another building. The walkway was lined with cypress trees and those cast iron street lamps with glass bulbs on top to illuminate the path at night. They were unlit now except by the quiet glow which came from the daylight resting in them. What light did they give at night? How dark and safe was this walkway? I walked up and down the walkway twice, looking very carefully from side to side and behind each bench and cypress tree then stopped and sat on a flat stone bench next to some scattered peanut shells. They lay broken open by something human or something rodent like, a squirrel or a rat.*

This the same piece with one or two changes but is there any difference, apart from the fact that it is written with 'I' instead of 'he?' The changes now make this an eyewitness account, something that happened to the person telling the story, which they witnessed and experienced personally and *want to tell us about*. Perhaps this seems to make the character's movements up the steps faster and the way he assesses the place seem more urgent and overall the whole piece appears quicker. This is something the narrator wants to tell us. It is important to tell us. This urgency draws us in. Compare the two versions and see if you agree.

The first person, eyewitness nature of this version illustrates both the strength and the weakness of first person writing. One of the strengths is the immediacy, the desire, the urge to communicate something. There is a story to tell and this person wants it to be heard. If they grab our attention, we will listen. One potential problem in all first person writing is that if you choose this mode to tell this story, then the 'I' character has to witness and experience everything in it. They cannot tell us about anything they do not know about, so that means they have to be present in every scene. That can be difficult to manage in terms of both the writing and the plotting and so hard to sustain in a convincing way. How does your character learn about events or conversations that they have not witnessed or been part of? A second difficulty with first person viewpoint can be that the reader wants to ask why they are being told this information at this time and why? As the first person narrator obviously knows the end, why don't they just 'cut to the chase' and tell us the ending? Why keep us waiting? If we get tired of the storyteller's voice, we might easily skip to the end. That is true of all writing but it is particularly so with first person. If you write in the first person, you have to make the narrators interesting, involving and arresting.

Let's try the same piece again in **third person omniscient viewpoint:**

> He walked up the steps cutting the steep lawns, past signs to the library where inside all its reading rooms the rows of bowed heads were already busy and the Schoenberg music block, where the second nervous student that morning was presenting his composition to the fearsome professor, and where two young female students were huddled in the rest room together, crying in advance of the treatment they would receive from the cruel maestro. He found the spot, the walkway between the library and another building. The walkway was lined with cypress trees that had once been specially imported from Greece and cast iron street lamps with Murano glass bulbs on top that the Dean, three deans ago, had raved about on his Grand Tour. They were unlit now except by the expensive glow which came from the daylight resting in them. He wondered what light they gave at night, particularly, how dark and safe this walkway was, without

knowing that in these more stringent times the institution's management had slashed the budget for lighting right across campus and that there had been a semester long campaign from the women's section of the students' union to get better lighting installed on this very spot because of a spate of attacks on females students. He walked up and down the walkway twice, looking very carefully from side to side and behind each bench and cypress tree then stopped and sat on a flat stone bench next to some scattered peanut shells that lay broken open by the squirrels that feasted there each evening on the bits of scattered food that always fell beneath the benches.

This is recognisably the same piece but with several noticeable differences. It does not matter whether it is better or worse in this form, but is it different? If you are unsure how it is different, read it again.

One difference is that it is quite a bit longer. That is because we are told a lot more. We are told about the background to the purchase of the lamps and the student union's concern about attacks on female students. We are also told about what is going on in the library and the music room. But let's look at it in terms of viewpoint. There are questions we can ask: if this was written in third person limited then we would ask how does the character know what is going on in the library as he passes? He might be able to see some of the bowed heads in the library windows as he goes by but is he capable of seeing inside *all* its reading rooms? And as for the Schoenberg music block where it is the 'second nervous student that morning' who is 'presenting his composition to the fearsome professor':

- How does he know it is the second student?
- How does he know exactly what the student is doing?
- How does he know that the professor is fearsome?

The scene continues: 'and where two young female students were huddled in the rest room together, crying in advance of the treatment they would receive from the cruel maestro.'

- How does he know there are two young females in the rest room? Has he been in there?
- How does he know they are huddled together crying?
- How does he know they are crying about the treatment they might get at the hands of the cruel maestro?
- Whose perception of the maestro is that he is cruel?

It would be possible to write this in limited viewpoint so that the character did know or could have observed it all but you would not write it in the way it is written above. The way the piece has been rewritten has to be omniscient narration.

Can you see and understand the difference? If not, then look again at all three viewpoint versions. If you do understand the difference, then you can ask the next question: does the piece of writing work better in third person limited, third person omniscient or first person? Different people will answer differently. It does not matter here, but whether a piece of writing works better in one mode or another is the sort of question you will find very helpful to apply to your own writing.

Key Idea

When you are trying to find the right voice for a piece of writing, try writing it in one voice then another to see what difference it makes to both the character and the narrative.

Write

Take from your writing, or write a new, brief scene in which a single character is performing an action and thinking. Do it in three different ways:

- First person
- Third person omniscient
- Third person limited.

Two hundred words are enough, though you might find the lengths vary according to the mode you use. Do it now.

- What did you learn?
- Did changing the viewpoint change the nature of the piece at all? How?
- Did it change the nature of the character and/or the story? How?
- Did it make you write different actions, and/or different thoughts in a particular mode?
- Did you prefer one version to another?
- If one version was longer than another why was that and what can you learn from it?

Key Idea

Viewpoint is a very subtle tool capable of adding a different dimension to character and to plot.

The unreliable narrator

Does your narrator always tell the truth?

It is very important to note that narrators, whether first or third person, can be reliable or unreliable; they can be telling us the truth or they can be spinning us a yarn. Which side of this coin you decide they are on can add interest to their character. Liars can be very engaging.

Dr James Sheppard, the narrator of Agatha Christie's first detective novel, *The Murder of Roger Ackroyd*, assists Poirot, a job done in later stories by Captain Hastings, not least because Sheppard turns out to be a very unreliable assistant and narrator indeed. He narrates this story for us and mainly through omitting to tell us the precise meaning of certain events and timings, or directing our attention away from important facts – a sort of literary sleight of hand – hides from us until the end of the story that he is in fact the murderer. Christie saw well the use to which she could put the viewpoint technique. Willkie Collins in *The Moonstone* used a 'multi narration' method with several voices telling us the story. This is rather like having witnesses at an accident making their statements. They all see the events differently, so that we experience the story told from various viewpoints that contradict each other; and the truth lies somewhere in between, for the detective to uncover.

The fact that certain characters only have certain limited views of events, limited by their knowledge, their ability to witness them or by their desires or prejudices, can work in a very helpful way in all stories, particularly when it comes to plotting, and especially with the dissemination and withholding of information. Much of the power of sensational novels and contemporary thrillers comes from fragmenting the narrative and doling the story out piece by piece to the readers through the fierce activity of some committed hero or heroine. Murder mystery writers, by having one limited viewpoint character, the detective, attempting to piece together a narrative through the method of interviewing and interpreting the answers and evasions of another set of limited viewpoint characters, build their stories around the opportunities presented by viewpoint. It is probably no accident that the whole murder mystery genre grew from a time when belief in the omniscient viewpoint was collapsing.

Murder mystery writers are basically handling the vagaries and shifting subtleties of a third person limited world. They are turning a technical exercise into engaging, enthralling writing. Each of the characters in a murder mystery has seen only part of the story at any one time and the detective tries to piece together a whole narrative from their fragmentary perceptions (or lies). A large amount of the very character and meaning of a murder mystery is built around an exploration of limited viewpoints, and this is not confined to that genre. A good deal of contemporary writing explores the piecemeal nature of limited viewpoint. Somewhere in the writer's head or notebook there may have been a complete narrative, but each of the characters in the story only has a part of it, and the story progresses by the bringing together of all those limited perceptions until the narrative is understood whole.

Key Idea

In a murder mystery, a slip in viewpoint can be used deliberately to show someone is lying or to muddy the narrative.

Case Study: Dr Watson

In the Sherlock Holmes stories, Doctor Watson is the viewpoint character. He writes down his and Sherlock Holmes' escapades. Giving Watson the pen was another masterly decision taken by Conan Doyle, both in characterization and in viewpoint. Watson is the filter and lens through which we view, witness and see in action the amazing character of Sherlock Holmes. He has the narrative voice. This is hugely important for the characters of both men. If Holmes had written about his own successes at solving crimes, if he had proclaimed his own genius, he would have been even more insufferable than he sometimes is. That Doctor Watson, the brave, honest, hero-worshipping, faithful Doctor Watson, narrates by far the huge majority of the stories, allows him to sing Holmes' praises in a way that makes Holmes more admirable, not less.

And Watson is very much the reliable narrator. He is good old English stock, born when gentlemen were gentlemen and the unreliable narrator was not the leading man in fiction. What Watson tells us we can believe and what he tells us about Holmes allows us to witness a genius at work.

Write

Choose one character to write about another character. Don't tell us about the narrator. Concentrate on the narrator's view of the subject and let their own character come through what they see and say about the other character. It could be husband on wife or vice versa, boss/employee, or whatever you like. The feeling for the other character might be love, admiration or loathing. Let the attitude come through the writing. (500 words)

THE SECONDARY CHARACTER

The secondary viewpoint character is also us, we the reader. This character can stand in for us at important moments in the narrative, asking the questions we would like to ask while also moving the narrative forward and so have an important relationship to the plot. Choosing a secondary character as the narrator of your story can be very important for the way the story is told and experienced and we will say more on this secondary viewpoint character in the next chapter.

10 TIPS FOR SUCCESS

1 *First person narration can be very immediate. We get to know the character well and are drawn into the story through the voice of the narrator.*

2 *Choosing the right viewpoint character can make the difference between a story that works and a story that fails.*

3 *Choosing a strong viewpoint character can give a story genuine impact.*

4 *In the third person limited mode, do not change your viewpoint character at odd moments or in the middle of scenes.*

5 *Be very careful to avoid slips of viewpoint. They can seriously destabilize your story.*

6 *If a story is not working in one viewpoint mode, try it in another.*

7 *Your narrator can be reliable or unreliable.*

8 *A secondary narrator can be very good at giving depth and charisma to a hero or heroine.*

9 *One way to create a genuine hero is to keep them at a distance, to filter them through the lens of someone more mortal.*

10 *The secondary narrator can stand in the reader's place, asking the sorts of questions readers want to ask about plot and character.*

10

Story concepts

In this chapter you will learn:
- a common way to structure a piece of writing
- the 'fish out of water' and the 'odd couple' story concepts
- the importance of secondary characters
- the dynamic relationship of character and plot.

A common way to structure a piece of writing

The recommended plan for an essay and also preparation for a talk is said to have three stages.

1 Start by telling your audience what you are going to do.
2 Do it.
3 Finish by telling them what you have done.

This also corresponds to the rational beginning, middle and end story model. It is in fact the model for the Teach Yourself series of books, of which this book is a part.

Look at any of the previous chapters in this book. Each time we have told you, the reader, at the start what the chapter was going to be about. 'In this chapter you will learn…' Then we have presented you with the substance of the chapter and at the end we have listed ten 'things to remember' in order to remind you the reader again what we covered in the chapter. This is such a common and accepted way of structuring information and it is intended to help us get information across. It is a good way of helping readers and learners pay attention and absorb information.

It is also used in the many reality television shows that flood our screens. A presenter will come on and say 'in this programme we are going to do this or that…' For example: 'A group of middle-aged men have been given a small budget each to buy second hand sports cars and race them against each other through a series of challenges to see which car remains the best.' Then we see the drivers out on location at a racetrack or perhaps somewhere in Antarctica or the Amazon take the cars through the challenges, usually a series of problems and complications that test both machine and driver until finally we go back to the studio for a recap where they declare a winner. Or a host will introduce us to contestants in a game show, the host will then explain the rules and what is at stake, we will see the contest, and the host will tell us at the end that we have a winner. Given that this way of structuring stories and events is so prevalent, it is probably not surprising that a lot of beginning creative writers have fallen into following this form without realizing it. The trouble is that the form might make for a good essay or talk, live or on television, but it spells death for a script or a piece of fiction. Creative writing is not, or is only ever partly, about giving people information or presenting an argument in the way that essays are.

Yet in structuring our creative work, particularly short pieces of prose and poems, the ideal essay/talk plan does seem to be deeply imbedded in people's psyches. Writers, particularly beginning writers, do often feel the need to give a preamble, echoing the idea of 'this is what I am going to do'. Then when they have finally got going, they write 'it' (the story, the play, the book, whatever it is) before – afraid the reader/viewer may still have missed the point – finally adding the bit which says, 'and this is what I have done'. So many short pieces offered in creative writing classes are like this where if the author just cut the first and last paragraphs and dived into the action, the writing would often be left much stronger for it. This is akin to what people mean when they 'plunge straight into the action'.

Similar problems can come up with the end as they do with the beginning. We can often go on too long, far longer than we should do. We have all read books and stories or seen films that are 'too long', which continue long after they are effectively over. The story is over but somehow the writer can't get off the stage. Like actors we should leave the audience wanting more, not less. But as writers, somehow we often can't resist just adding that little bit more of an explanation. This probably again comes out of weakness or uncertainty about our craft; we are afraid, we lack confidence in what we have written and we add a bit more just in case our point has not got across. We can fail to let the writing speak for itself.

Key Idea

A piece of writing can speak for itself – our job as writers is to let it.

You can always find out later if where you have started is the right place to start. That is one way that writing is different to a journey. Once you have started on a journey you can't revise your departure point. In writing, you can.

Key Idea

You can find what to write through writing. You can find where to begin through beginning.

As for the end, a little cutting, even as little as a small incision, can make such a difference to a piece of work. It has worked wonders for any number of short stories and poems in writing classes. Try it for yourself.

Write

Take a short piece of writing you have done (poem, story, script).

- Cut off the first few lines of the poem, or a paragraph or two of the story, or a scene of the script.
- Cut a similar amount from the end (the first and last pages even).
- How does it read?
- Has it brought any detail or character to life?
- Is the piece better in this new form?

If you like this new form, then you might like to keep the work like that. If not, if it has damaged it too much, then put it back the way it was – the magic of writing is that change is not fixed.

Key Idea

You can change things in your writing, yes, and if the changes don't work, you can put it all back again the way it was. But give the changes a chance to work.

Case Study: Trimming

A student asked in a writing class to do the trimming exercise went home and did it. When she came back she said that it had improved the work no end, but after a little while the tiny worm of doubt crept into her brain and she began to look at the new beginning and end. When she came back the next week she said 'I realized that what I had left was the new first and last paragraphs and the more I looked at them the more I wondered if they were necessary too, so I cut those too.' Now she did not know where to stop. She had unleashed a virus that was eating up her work. She was someone who knitted and her writing was in some ways like her knitting. It felt to her that a piece of knitting was dropping its stitches from both ends and soon it would unravel into nothing but the original ball of wool. She needed reassurance that to stop was ok.

Key Idea

If you have actually started your story at a later point instead of what you thought was the start, then cut the chapters or scenes or move the scenes to the start, or even swap chapters over. Do whatever works to make the story work. And if the changes don't work, put it all back the way it was.

In doing all of this you will be spending your words wisely and the words you spend will mean more. They will mean more to you and mean more to your readers. But in terms of how to give a story a framework, let's turn to ideas more suited to creative writing.

How many plots are there?

According to who you read or listen to there are x number of plots for stories. The number 36 has been a favourite ever since the nineteenth century when Georges Polti produced a famous book called *The Thirty-six Dramatic Situations* in which he attempted to categorize every dramatic situation that could occur in a story or a performance. This book is still published today. Christopher Booker's book *The Seven Basic Plots* (2004) says, you guessed it, that there are seven basic plots. Some comedy writers say there are only two basic stories, the 'fish out of water' and the 'odd couple'. In many ways it does not matter what number people come up with, but the idea that a lot of stories boil down to certain key, basic components is a useful one. From the practical point of the writer, two can be quite enough.

THE FISH OUT OF WATER

The 'fish out of water' theme is centred on character and place, the idea that everyone belongs somewhere and needs to belong somewhere and that if you take them out of that place, then the character is disorientated and tested. A disorientated and tested character can develop situations that can be developed into stories and plots.

Key Idea

We both *form* and *carry* place with us. Even the homeless, displaced characters in Samuel Beckett's *Waiting for Godot* carry their histories with them.

If a character is at home this sense of place is with them, perhaps unnoticed because they don't need to note it, they just live it. But a character that is away from home stands out more, even if it is only in their own minds because they are at odds with their environment. They are different, both in themselves and to the place in which they find themselves. They are different not only because they may not speak the language, or they dress differently but because they feel different inside. They might be excited about being somewhere different or they may feel the opposite. They may be in a different place because they were ejected from the place where they belong; the new place may not be something they either chose or like. Wherever they are and whatever the reasons for being there, they carry with them all the attributes that have come to make them who and what they are. Accents, habits and the way we dress, what we own and have and want, all define us as people. Place defines us too.

We can all miss home when we are away from it and feel it acutely. We can feel it as a disadvantage. Maybe the way we dress and cook and eat back home is not the way people dress and cook and eat in the new place and that makes us stand out. Maybe some of the ways we dress and talk and act seem gauche and old fashioned or uncool so that we stand out and do not blend in. The drive not to stand out can be a strong character and story motive. Characters that love being away from home and see being in a new place as an exciting new challenge can still be fish out of water.

 ## Key Idea

A strong character motive will always be a strong plot or story motive. Anything a character wants or needs or desires will give a plot twists, drives and problems. When a character is in a strange place in their lives, the sense of usual place can be even stronger. Getting back to a place from which they have been ripped or torn is a strong character motive which can lead to strong plot drives.

In the film *E.T.*, the line 'E.T. phone home' was about all the alien could say at first. Being separated from his own people, being lost in an alien world, gave him the very strong drive to get back there. He was a fish out of water and this drive and the drive of the children, who found him and helped him, gave the film its drive. In Homer's *The Odyssey*, Odysseus strives through many different adventures in order to return home, where he finds his faithful wife and dog are waiting for him. It is a natural and basic urge for people to want to be where they belong. Characters taken out of their environment, the place they belong, strive to get back there or to adapt better to the new place.

Key Idea

The drive to get home is an immensely powerful one, much used in writing, but it still has a lot of power in it to be used again in new stories yet to be written.

The desire to get out of one place and one sort of existence into a better place and a better existence is one of the basic character and story drives. As a writer, when you take someone out of their usual world and throw them into another and see how they get on, you are working with the 'fish out of water' story theme. You will write scenes which try to keep them in this new environment for the duration of the story because if they get back to their world easily and too early, then there is no story. Being a fish out of water, the character has problems to overcome and problems mean action and reaction. Action and reaction mean stories.

Case Study: The Shawshank Redemption

In many ways the 1994 cult movie *The Shawshank Redemption* is a fish out of water story. The main character, Andy Dufresne, is wrongly imprisoned for the murder of his wife. He does not belong in his new environment – prison – and he strives throughout the film to overcome all the obstacles put in his path and to clear his name.

Andy Dufresne illustrates many of the problems faced by a fish out of water character. First, he has to acclimatize himself to his new environment and second, survive in it because the new world is often a dangerous place. Third, he has to turn this new world around in such a way that he can use it for his own purposes and ultimate goal. In *The Shawshank Redemption*, Andy Dufresne moves from accepting the new world he is in, to overcoming the violent attacks of the inmates, to dealing with the governor using him in a money laundering enterprise, to ultimately escaping. The drive to get out is at the heart of his character and therefore at the heart of the film.

Key Idea

The drive of fish out of water characters is basic: to survive and, if they can survive, to then thrive.

Fish need water to live. It is their natural environment. Without it they die. The struggle to survive is an incredible drive. What could be stronger than it? Taken out of a place where they are settled and where they belong a character struggles. If characters are to be able to live in the new and hostile world in which they find themselves, they have to make this new world habitable or at least survivable for them, and through their struggles they discover new qualities in themselves and often thrive. Writers have exploited these needs throughout the history of storytelling.

Case Study: Legally Blonde

With her pink clothes and fluffy manner, Elle Woods, the lead character in *Legally Blonde*, is a fish out of water. Elle does not belong in the new Harvard Law environment she enters but after some difficult challenges and setbacks she flourishes and wins through. Identifying the place a character comes from and the role they played there is vital to defining who and what the fish out of water is and what the struggle will be in their new world. Andy Dufresne in *The Shawshank Redemption* was a banker before he was sent to prison and he uses his banking knowledge and skills to carve a new role for himself in prison, a role that ultimately allows him the freedom to plan and execute his escape. In *Legally Blonde*, Elle Woods uses her knowledge of fashion, shoes and the manicurist's art to win a prestigious legal case in her new environment. By using her previously acquired knowledge of shoes and shampoo and make-up, she successfully demolishes a witness testimony in a crucial court case. The place she comes from has equipped her with the knowledge and skills that she uses to triumph in her new world. Had she been someone who belonged at Harvard, she would have been like everyone else who belonged there and would not have seen the weak spot in the witness testimony. Without coming from her own particular place and entering the new world she would not have had the struggle and the triumph, but nor would she have had the skills to adapt and survive and we would not have had the story to enjoy.

The two distinct worlds, as well as the fish out of water theme, are neatly and cleverly captured in the title, *Legally Blonde*. Being blonde, she was supposed to be stupid. She proved she was bright and more than capable. She used the way of thinking from her own world to give her useful insights in her new world; she became a great student, potentially a great lawyer and a great blonde.

Case Study: Working Girl

The same use of the skills and insights gained in her ordinary world to triumph in her new world can be seen in the fish out of water character, Tess, in the 1988 film *Working Girl*. A Staten Island raised secretary, Tess admires her new female boss in the mergers and acquisitions department of a Wall Street investment bank and wants to be like her. By aspiring to better herself she is already psychologically on the brink of moving out of the ordinary world in which she starts. She has a boyfriend who is very happy with where he is, but she has glimpsed the possibility of another, better world. The push comes when she finds her boyfriend in bed with another woman. She goes to stay temporarily at her female boss's house in Manhattan while her boss is away. The psychological dislocation has now become both emotional and physical. But there is a fresh betrayal for her when she discovers that her boss has stolen her idea for a major business deal. The new world is not that safe either and to survive in it she will have to fight. She determines to pull the deal off herself though totally out of her depth in this new corporate world. In the end she triumphs, and the key thing that turns the tables in her favour is the knowledge she brought with her from her ordinary world; a knowledge which came from reading the down-market magazines that were part of her previous Staten Island character. Such material was so far beneath her boss that she would never have seen the insights it offered.

The lead character of the 1994 film *My Cousin Vinny* is another fish out of water character that uses the skills gained from his Brooklyn background to triumph in a testing court case in the Deep South.

Key Idea

Remember that in a 'fish out of water' story, a character takes their sense of place with them. They can either lose it or leave it behind or they can use where they come from and the knowledge and skills they have gained there, to transform their position in the new world that they have entered.

Often stories built around the fish out of water theme end up with an exciting mix of the two worlds the character inhabits. The character draws on knowledge and skills gained in their previous world to take on and overcome important obstacles in the new world and in doing so make an exciting meld of their past and present worlds. If you have never thought about it or used it, the fish out of water device is something worth spending time on. It is a staple theme of comedy and more serious story genres too. The lead character from *Gladiator*, once he becomes a fish out water in the world of the gladiator, uses the skills he gained as a soldier and a general to survive and ultimately triumph. The fish out of water theme is present in *The Tempest* when Ferdinand and his crew are shipwrecked on the island controlled by Prospero, and in *Twelfth Night* where Viola is shipwrecked on the shores of Illyria and has to assume the identity of a young pageboy, Cesario, for the bulk of the play.

Hitchcock's *North by Northwest* has a lightness of touch that borders on the comic and the Cary Grant character is definitely a fish out of water as his character is taken out of his ordinary world of advertising and thrown into another strange, new world of espionage. The film *A Fish called Wanda* actually has the word fish in the title. In this film, the John Cleese character is the fish out of water as he is thrown from his straight world as a lawyer into the world of thieves and robbers, lured by the sexy femme fatale, played by Jamie Lee Curtis. *Trading Places*, the 1983 film, has Eddie Murphy and Dan Ackroyd as characters poles apart – one a vagrant, the other a successful commodities broker – who trade places, each becoming a fish out of water in the new worlds into which they are thrust.

Write

Using one of the characters from a piece you are already working on or have finished, or taking one of the characters developed through exercises in this book, establish a normal world for them in a scene or two and then plunge them into another, very different world that will challenge and threaten them. Give them a strong desire to get back to their previous world and/or problems and obstacles in their new world. Challenge them and see what decisions they take in the face of the different obstacles they have. (1000 words)

THE ODD COUPLE

Neil Simon's clever, funny 1965 play *The Odd Couple* is built around a very odd couple: Oscar Madison, a recently divorced sportswriter and a slob played in the 1968 film by Water Matthau, and Felix Ungar, a hypochondriac news writer whose marriage is ending and who is fastidious in the extreme, played in the film by Jack Lemmon.

Odd couples are often characters from very different backgrounds and temperaments who have somehow been thrown together. Having little in common with each other, they are yoked together in such a way that they cannot easily separate themselves. In their struggles with each other they spark off each other and this generates a story.

But the odd couple theme has been a staple of comedic and more serious writing for a lot longer than since the 1960s. Katherine and Petruchio are an odd couple in Shakespeare's *Taming of the Shrew*, as are Titania and Bottom in *A Midsummer Night's Dream*. That play in fact is riddled with odd couples, all in love with the wrong person: Helena is in love with Demetrius and Hermia is in love with Lysander but at different times in the play, Lysander is in love with both Hermia and Helena, while Demetrius is in love with Hermia and Helena. The odd couplings make for some funny comic scenes and give dynamic forward movement to the story.

Hal and Falstaff form an odd couple in the *Henry IV and V* plays. Estragon and Vladimir, the two characters in Samuel Beckett's *Waiting for Godot* are an odd couple, as are the two characters in another Beckett play, *Happy Days*. The 1960s sitcom *Steptoe and Son* was a classic example of an odd couple situation; the son and father tied together, always fighting and desperate to get away from each other, yet knowing they are tied to each other for good. Mel Gibson and Danny Glover form an odd couple relationship in *Lethal Weapon*. Other examples: Jeeves and Wooster; Holmes and Watson. There have been numerous films where the human actor shares the lead with an animal: a dog in *Turner and Hooch*, and an orang-utan in the 1978 film *Every Which Way But Loose*. *Thelma and Louise* is an odd couple story. Frasier Crane and his father are an odd couple in the sitcom *Frasier*. Think of the many stories you have read or seen where, at the heart, you have an unlikely pair.

Sometimes you get 'odd couple' relationships within a fish out of water story. The two main characters in *Trading Places* are an odd couple as well as being in a fish out of water movie. You could argue that the relationship between the lead character, Andy Dufresne, and Ellis 'Red' Redding, the prisoner who befriends him in *The Shawshank Redemption* is an odd couple relationship, or has elements of an odd couple relationship, even though it is within the overall frame of a fish out of water story. The same can be said of the relationship of Vinny and the judge trying the case against Vinny's cousin in *My Cousin Vinny*.

Case Study: My Cousin Vinny

My Cousin Vinny is about a Brooklyn ex-mechanic Vinny becoming a lawyer. Vinny is not a criminal lawyer, yet for his first case he takes on the job of defending two young men, one of whom is his cousin, against a charge of murder. The film revolves around Vinny and his developmental experience of the trial which is held in the Deep South. Vinny is a fish out of water both in the South and in the courtroom. But this is not the main element of the story. Central to the film is the odd couple relationship Vinny has with the judge trying the case. Judge Chamberlain Haller is anxious that a big city lawyer like Vinny will look down his nose at a backwoods Southern court. He tests and obstructs Vinny all the way, forcing Vinny to call on all his innate skills at argument and to develop the new skills required to triumph in a court of law. Vinny and the judge are worthy adversaries, an odd couple who reach a mutual respect at the end of the film. Once that moment of respect is achieved, the story is over and the film ends. Vinny has been a willing pupil and has learned a good deal from his antagonistic tutor/mentor, the judge.

The odd couple relationship can be antagonistic. It can be between an antagonist and protagonist, but it can also be between friends.

The importance of secondary characters

THE HERO AND BUDDY

The relationship that the buddy character has with the main character is quite often an odd couple relationship. Some of the most famous duos in films and stories are odd couples. Think of Batman and Robin or Nick and Nora Charles, a married couple from the *Thin Man* series of films in the 1930s, who solved crimes while bantering. As we commented in the previous chapter, when creating the character of Sherlock Holmes, Conan Doyle gave Holmes a number two, and in doing this Doyle created an archetypal odd couple.

The number two, the loyal friend, the sounding-board against which the lead character of the detective can bounce ideas, discuss the case and so on, has become a staple of murder mystery fiction. Holmes and Watson, Poirot and Hastings, Lord Peter Wimsey and Harriet Vane, Dalziel and Pascoe, Morse and Lewis… these are just a few of the crime fighting odd couples that writers have created. It is also common in comedy. The relationship of Vinny and his fiancée Mona Lisa Vito in *My Cousin Vinny* is also that of a hero and a buddy character, or a sidekick.

There is a similar duo in another wonderful comic creation by P. G. Wodehouse, that of Jeeves and Wooster. Looking at this odd couple allows us to make another valuable point. Bertie Wooster always takes up much more space in the Jeeves and Wooster stories. Why is that? If Jeeves is the clever and resourceful one, as he always proves in the stories, why does he not dominate the narrative? Well in fact he does dominate the narrative with his personality, but why is he not on every page? The answer is that this is very much a case of less is more. It is exactly the same with Holmes and Watson. Genius needs distance.

We can get near to Holmes through Watson's mediation in a way that we would not be able to approach Holmes himself. The sun of Holmes would burn too brightly for us. It is only as it is mediated through the lens of Watson's pen – if a pen can be said to have a lens – that we are able to share in Holmes' genius.

If Jeeves and Holmes were on every page of the stories in which they feature, we would get tired of them. Worse, we would get to know them too well and thus their genius would be reduced. Both Conan Doyle and P. G. Wodehouse knew this. In *The Hound of the Baskervilles* Holmes appears right at the start, accepts the case and then says he is too busy in London with other matters to leave immediately and sends Watson down to Dartmoor in his stead. But unbeknownst to Watson and the reader, Holmes does go down to Dartmoor. He disguises himself as a tramp and camps out on the moors some distance from the house, watching Watson at Baskerville Hall struggling to make sense of it all. For two-thirds of the narrative Holmes is absent, leaving Doctor Watson, pistol in hand, to carry the narrative. Holmes only appears at the end to provide the solution and wrap up the mystery. Jeeves provides a similar role in the countless Jeeves and Wooster stories.

Jeeves steps out of the narrative early on, usually because Bertie has upset him by wanting to wear something totally inappropriate or to play the banjolele (on which occasion Jeeves actually leaves Bertie's employ), and Bertie is left to his own devices to solve the most complicated of matters. Of course they only get worse because Bertie is inept. It is only at the end when Jeeves relents and floats back into the picture to provide the answer that everything is resolved and order restored. One has the sense of Jeeves in the offing, observing it all and waiting for his moment to come back in to set the world to rights in his god-like manner.

Holmes, too, is the genius who steps in late in the day with the answer to the story puzzle. As such he is someone sure to retain his mystery and mystique and above all his power. If we as readers were to spend too long with Holmes, we would start to know him too well and his power as a character would be reduced. Both Holmes and Jeeves need to be kept at a distance, like a god, because that way they retain their mystery. We mere humans cannot get too close to gods; they are gods. Nick Carraway, the narrator of *The Great Gatsby*, plays a similar intermediary role with the wealthy, mysterious and enigmatic character of Jay Gatsby, though Gatsby is not a god. But what helps the characters keep this distance is the choice of viewpoint character.

Key Idea

Choosing a secondary character as your narrator can help make your main character interesting, enigmatic and even strong.

The sidekick is a necessary part of the hero or heroine's characters and of the stories that feature them. The sidekick or buddy character has a vital role in character and plot. They have to carry the bulk of the narrative, allowing the hero to shine. We can spend time with the fallible, human, ordinary, likeable second character. But if we saw too much of the genius or hero, we would begin to know him too well. This would bring him down to our level and make him less of a genius.

WRITING STRONG MAIN CHARACTERS

If you are going to develop a strong, powerful heroic figure, they will be stronger and more powerful if you show them through the eyes of a good, well-rounded secondary character. The relationship between the lead character or hero and the good friend, or second banana, needs to be a close one – a good one. They need to have sympathy with each other as well as a certain friction, even antagonism. The black and white *Thin Man* series of films, mentioned previously, had Dick Powell and Myrna Loy playing a comedy crime-cracking duo who were married, and this allowed their detecting to have the necessary warmth and antagonism of any good marriage. Holmes and Watson have a relationship akin to marriage. There is a by-play that goes on, the sort of by-play that exists in an old, established relationship.

Holmes quite often sets Watson up as a sort of fall guy for his own and our benefit. He does this right at the beginning of *The Hound of the Baskervilles* when he asks Watson to apply his famous method of deduction to a walking stick that an as-yet-unnamed visitor has left behind. Watson, like a good and dutiful dog, obliges, makes deductions and gets it all wrong. Holmes then takes over and shows Watson where he went wrong. He says Watson shines a light, praising him, while mocking him because he says that Watson shines a light in the wrong place, thus allowing Holmes to see where the truth is. The first chapter of *The Hound of the Baskervilles* is a very good piece of comic writing, establishing the hero/loyal buddy relationship, and also sending up the whole Holmes–Watson dialectic. It is also a good example of how a writer might perform character deduction from something as simple as a walking stick.

But moments of play like this, or the ones that go on between Jeeves and Wooster, are not enough to create heroic characters or sustain a plot.

The dynamic relationship of character and plot

What makes Sherlock Holmes a great detective is not the fact that he is one half of a dynamic odd couple. It is not the little set pieces with Watson, amusing though they are, nor is it his unique appearance. Ultimately what makes Sherlock Holmes a great detective is the fact that he solves crimes.

What would it matter what he looked like if Holmes failed in his *raison d'être*: to be a detective and to solve crimes? Detectives detect. We forget that Columbo looks a mess because he is so dynamic in his job. If he were hopeless at his job, we would have no story and no character. All of the characters we have briefly looked at in this book say the same thing – that a character is nothing outside of the dynamic of a story. And they also say that it is the dynamics of the characters that actually create the stories.

When we look back at the question with which this book started – which is most important, character or plot? The answer is becoming evident: they are both important. Character and plot are inseparably linked. As the song goes, 'you can't have one without the other'.

 ## Key Idea

A character needs action, needs to do, needs a plot in which he can come to life, otherwise he is an assemblage of so much detail that remains lifeless and still born.

Holmes' cape will hang on the back of the door, his deerstalker on the peg, both empty until Holmes the man puts them on and gets to work. Similarly Holmes' rooms, packed with detail as they are, would remain empty as a museum without the living, breathing character to make use of all the everyday items from the chairs and books to the train timetables. Without the character to animate and bring it to life, any setting is dead. A character needs to act and do and speak to live. However well constructed, put together and described, character and setting needs the plot to bring it to life.

Key Idea

We could rewrite Descartes' famous statement – 'I think therefore I am' – for characters in our stories: 'I speak, I act therefore I am.'

Sherlock Holmes has undoubted energy. He also has periods of ennui where he sits in his rooms, doped and lethargic, but he comes to life when he has a case that grips him. He is like all character creations, inert until they are called to action. What makes a character spring to life is how they act, what they do and how that acts on the plot. All this brings out qualities of character that even they may not have known about.

Vinny in *My Cousin Vinny*, although initially totally inexperienced in court procedure, by calling on his new knowledge and using the skills of his old, familiar world of being able to argue, triumphs. Whether you are going to write a fish out of water story or an odd couple story, you have to add the dynamism that comes from putting your characters into situations where they have to strive, where they are able to achieve – and so generate a story and a plot.

Case Study: The African Queen

What we might call the 'two halves of a life' also collide in *The African Queen*, the novel by C. S. Forester, later made into a classic film starring Humphrey Bogart and Katherine Hepburn. The Hepburn character, Rose, is a very spirited, quite religious woman, the sister, servant and companion to her brother Samuel, an Anglican missionary in Central Africa during World War I. When Samuel dies, Rose is alone until an Englishman (changed to a Canadian in the film to accommodate Bogart's accent) named Allnut arrives. He is the mechanic and skipper of the African Queen, a rough man and a drunkard. Again the plot forces these two characters together and provides them with situations that force reactions from them. That these two opposites end up falling in love is a blend only achieved through their jointly facing the severe obstacles of a long journey down river as well as an encounter with a ship of the German navy. The Allnut character accesses more of a spiritual inner life as he falls in love and learns to care for Rose and the qualities she demonstrates, and she correspondingly moves in his direction as she learns not to fear his rough-edged masculinity. The two very different sides that they represent come together through the action of the story. It is always the action of the story that forces the characters to achieve this movement, this blend of different views and ways of negotiating the world. In *The African Queen*, the two characters – representing the earthly and the spiritual – reach some sort of reconciliation through the workings of plot and character. This movement between conflict and resolution is at the core of the vital relationship between plot and character.

You don't just write the character then come up with the plot. Character and plot are intimately connected and grow together. Plot situations make demands on the people in your stories, which in turn force decisions or actions out of them. They make demands on them to perform actions and say words that reveal character. Characters also make choices that affect and determine plot changes and outcomes. Once you have a living, breathing, argumentative character, you have someone who is going to help you shape the plot.

 ## Key Idea

Characters can work solo against their opponents, or they can work as a duo, in the manner of Holmes and Watson, but whether they are in 'fish out of water' or 'odd couple' stories, they have to work hard for you.

 ## Write

At each stage of this exercise, make sure you write straight away before going on to the next instruction.

- Create a protagonist, or main character, in 100 words. Make them sympathetic, someone readers will care about and establish them in a convincing setting. Write it now. (100 words)
- Now, give them a want or need. (100 words)
- Give them a big problem – something or someone is preventing them getting what they want or need. This could be another person, themselves or a natural event. If you choose another person, create them and make them a fully rounded and strong opponent (antagonist). (100 words)
- Now, bring the two into conflict. (100 words)

- Your protagonist (your hero or heroine) attempts to overcome the obstacle. (100 words)
- They fail. (100 words)
- They try again. (100 words)
- They fail. (100 words)
- They try to overcome the obstacles again. (100 words)
- This time they succeed. Or if they fail at the goal, they succeed in another way, i.e. they learn something about themselves and are a changed person, for the better (and this turns out to be the real goal all along).

How did it turn out? Can you develop, tidy it up and turn it into a finished story? Try.

1   *Many stories can be classified as a 'fish out of water' or 'odd couple' concept.*

2   *The fish out of water and odd couple devices are staple themes of comedy and more serious story genres too.*

3   *Being out of their usual environment gives characters huge problems to overcome. Having problems to overcome is what forces a story to grow.*

4   *A displaced character will have a very strong drive to get back what they have lost.*

5   *Characters carry with them all that they are, including a sense of place, and place can contribute to make characters what they are.*

6   *Characters need goals, desires and obstacles in order to generate energy and life in themselves and in a plot.*

7   *A strong character motive will always be a strong plot or story motive. Anything a character wants or needs or desires will give a plot twists, drives and problems.*

8   *The desire to get out of one place and one sort of existence into a better place and a better existence is one of the basic character and story drives.*

9   *Odd couples are characters from very different backgrounds and temperaments who have somehow been thrown together and who cannot easily separate themselves.*

10 *Creating an odd couple by putting two distinctive characters together and seeing how they spark off each other can be a good way of developing situations – and situations can develop into stories.*

11

Genre and plot

In this chapter you will learn:

- techniques that other writers use
- about crafting genre and plot
- about the demands of genre
- how to let go of your characters and your work.

Learning from other writers

It is not only helpful to look at our own writing to help ourselves to learn, but essential to look at what other writers have done and try to discover what their strengths and weaknesses are.

 ## Key Idea

Once you start writing, you need to read as a writer not as a reader. Look at a writer you like to see how they do it. If you know some of their techniques, you can try to emulate them.

WHICH SHOULD YOU START WITH, CHARACTER OR PLOT?

Certain writers in certain genres start more with plot than with character. The James Bond films start with action: a dramatic, exciting action scene, after which they pull back to sketch in some character and some story. There are other writers for whom plot is the important thing and character is a part of the mechanics of telling the story. Characters in these stories are often two-dimensional: flat, not round.

Agatha Christie was inspired to write her first detective story by a challenge from her sister who bet Agatha that she could not write something that her sister could not guess the end of before she got there. To that competitive sisterly exchange the world owes *The Mysterious Affair at Styles* and the entire Agatha Christie oeuvre that followed. Agatha Christie started and continued with plot: the mechanics of who did what to whom and when. She wanted to trick her reader and hold back the big secret, of whodunit, until the last possible moment. For her, writing detective fiction was to create a puzzle, pure and complex. The whole genre of the classical detective novel in fact is built around this puzzle element, the game, the competition between writer and reader. Certain readers love a clever, inventive writer who can outwit them; the cleverer the better because this reflects on them as a reader. If they can't guess the ending, then the writer is very smart; if it is a smart piece of writing but they do guess the ending of it, then the reader can take a pat on the back, it shows how clever they are. A good, well-plotted crime, thriller or murder mystery is win–win for writer and reader and publisher.

In the genre of detective fiction or murder mystery, characters often come secondary to plot and are often twisted to fit the plot needs. If you have a strongly plotted story, you need to be able to move people about and fit them in to suit your requirements, and if your characters are strong and individual and capable of talking back to you and saying they don't want to be put in this or that scenario, then they can make the plotting difficult. You can end up either straining the plot or straining the character. If you have ever thought the characters in a golden age detective novel remain somewhat pale and two-dimensional, perhaps it is because they need to be. They need to serve the plot and don't need to have three-dimensional lives of their own. We might even say they *should not* have three-dimensional lives of their own, for if they did they would resist being moved about in a way that serves the plot. They might talk back and say no. The only characters with three-dimensional lives in crime and murder mystery stories are the detective and their sidekick. The others are formed of various degrees of flatness.

Raymond Chandler once said that when he hit a problem in the story, he would have a man come into the room with a gun in his hand. This is something of a throwaway remark, obviously, but as it often is with amusing remarks, there is a truth at the heart of it. Having something dramatic like a man come into the room with a gun in his hand is a good way to increase tension in a story. A man with a gun in his hand immediately spells threat and danger and perks up a reader's interest. Such a plot device could also gloss over any number of holes in a story and there can be big holes in these sorts of stories.

Among Chandler's novels, *The Big Sleep*, the first of his books about the private eye Philip Marlowe, is known for its convoluted plot. In it, Marlowe is hired by a wealthy General Sternwood to get his daughter out of trouble. When the Sternwoods' chauffeur, Owen Taylor, is found dead in the harbour, apparently having driven off the pier and drowned, the doctor suspects the cause of death could be a blow to the back of the head. When the book was adapted for the screen, it was pulled apart by the screenwriters, director and actors. This is a necessary part of the process of adaptation. In such dialogue with the original material, questions come up and inconsistencies are spotted. In the filming of *The Big Sleep*, no one apparently could work out who killed the chauffeur. Had he died by accident, killed himself or been murdered? The director, Howard Hawks, could not work it out. Three screenwriters are credited, including William Faulkner. They did not know. Someone contacted Chandler, he told a friend in a later letter: 'They sent me a wire

… asking me, and dammit I didn't know either.' The plot was so convoluted even the author could not unpick it! Does it matter, you might ask? It clearly did not stop *The Big Sleep* being published and selling. It is now recognized as a classic.

But if you are going to use a device such as 'man enters with gun in hand' to raise the stakes, you need to consider what would happen if the character with the gun says no: 'No, I am not coming in with a gun in my hand.' Or if he says: 'I don't carry a gun. I might come in with a bunch of flowers or the latest gardening magazine. That is more true to my character.' What Raymond Chandler would have done then, presumably, was get another guy with a gun to come in and bump off the guy with the flowers. Character is definitely subservient to plot when it is used like this. You want a flat, one-dimensional character coming through that door with a gun, someone expendable, not a fully rounded, three-dimensional character we can get to know and care about. This is character as plot device.

P. D. James claims to have known from a very early age that she wanted to be a crime writer because when she was read the nursery rhyme of Humpty Dumpty – 'Humpty Dumpty sat on a wall, Humpty Dumpty had a great fall…' she wanted to know 'did he fall or was he pushed?' It's a good story and Ms James uses it to good effect at talks to crime writers to make her audience laugh, but there is probably some truth in it too. Writers have an instinct for the sort of pieces they want to write and the area they want to work in. They know what feels right for them.

Stephen King, when he began to sit down and write, let his instinct as well as his talent and his imagination take him naturally down the path of horror and suspense. He belongs to these genres as much as they now belong to him.

Alfred Hitchcock worked in a genre, or, as great artists do, maybe he established a genre of his own. Something can now be labelled 'Hitchcockian' and we know what that means. Such a piece of work will probably have a huge element of suspense in it; it could display a macabre wit. It could contain an icy blonde in peril and have a hero both ordinary and extraordinary.

The interrelationship of character and plot is fundamentally important to a Hitchcock movie. He likes to take a character and establish them in their ordinary world before he pitches them into an unusual or extraordinary world. He wants to see what happens to a character, to test them and see what it brings out of them. As we discussed earlier, the film *North by Northwest* is a good example of this.

Case Study: North by Northwest

The main character, Roger Thornhill, played by Cary Grant, is an advertising executive. At the start of the film, Roger Thornhill goes to a hotel for a drink with a group of other advertising men and by accident is mistaken for a Mr Caplan. He is immediately kidnapped by two armed men and taken to a house of a Mr Lester Townsend where he is confronted by a suave and mysterious man, who questions him as if he were a CIA or FBI agent. Thornhill naturally denies he is Mr Caplan at which point the suave man, played by James Mason, orders the men who kidnapped him to kill Thornhill. They do this by pouring a bottle of bourbon down his throat and putting him behind the wheel of a car on a steep hill. Thornhill evades death but ends up in court for drink driving. Trying to prove his innocence he returns to the house of Mr Lester Townsend with the police where they find no evidence to back up Thornhill's story. When the police in fact discover that Lester Townsend is addressing the UN assembly, they think that Thornhill simply drank too much and spun a lie to cover himself. Determined to prove his innocence, determination being one of the mainsprings of character, he goes to the UN building where he talks to the real Lester Townsend. Before Thornhill can ask him any more, Townsend is killed. Thornhill is thought to be the assassin and runs. The film then travels across America with Thornhill eluding police and the FBI, trying to catch up with the real Mr Caplan and spending the night in a Pullman couchette with a glamorous Hitchcock-type, icy blonde double agent that he falls for. This is what can happen to the ordinary, every man thrown from one world into another, Hitchcock is saying. Ordinary men can become heroes when they are pitched into extraordinary worlds.

It would be interesting to know whether Hitchcock started with character or plot. It is known that he spent a long time working with his writers planning and developing the stories he filmed so that the finished piece had a tightly plotted story as well as good, believable characters. Hitchcock wanted that important balance. He did not want to make what he called 'ice-box movies'. These were films that he said worked in the cinema; they worked all the way home; they worked while you parked the car in the garage and walked into the house. They worked right up until the moment when you opened the fridge or 'icebox' door and reached in for a glass of milk before going to bed and at that point you thought,

'Hang on a minute… why didn't the hero or heroine call the police or pick up the gun or shut the door, or…? And this moment, the 'ice-box moment' Hitchcock said, was when the plot fell to pieces and the film stopped working. It had kept you on the edge of your seat in the cinema but after a short period of reflection when everything began to sink in, its flaws had become clear and it had come to be seen more as a guilty pleasure than a joy. The interaction of character and plot, that important balance and how we achieve that successfully in our work is the subject of our book. Hitchcock is an excellent example of how a great artist worked at achieving that.

CHARACTER TO GENRE PLOT

The following exercise will be followed by a discussion of genre, which highlights some of the elements of genre such as atmosphere, characters, goals and desires and the special world of the genre. First, let's be clear what we mean by genre. By genre we mean 'a particular type or kind of literature, music or other artistic work' (*Chambers 21st Century Dictionary*). We mean, for example, science fiction, murder mystery, horror or suspense. And there are many others. They will have a 'special world' that immediately characterizes the stories in the genre of science fiction, murder mystery or whatever. Keeping the thoughts about the special world and its unique characteristics in mind, try the following exercise and write it either as a ghost story, murder mystery, sci-fi, or other genre of your choice.

Study this list of jobs, professions and roles:

coachman	alien	astronaut	explorer	soldier
policeman	priest	princess	doctor	scientist
detective	murderer	victim	vampire	lover
ghost	prostitute	judge	housekeeper	highwayman

You are now going to write a piece of genre fiction.

Write

Pick a genre and, keeping your choice of genre in mind, be it ghost story, vampire story, murder mystery, etc., choose one of the occupations or professions from the list above and get ready to write from the point of view of that person in the special world of the genre. This exercise has a series of steps, and surprise is important in this exercise, so make sure you cover up what is below before you continue. The exercise will work best if you do not know what is coming in the next step. It may mean that you introduce something in one stage and have to do a complete turnaround in the next stage. Go with it; see if you can make it connect and work. Test yourself and your powers of invention.

When you uncover each new request (labelled 1, 2, 3, etc.) write quickly and under time pressure, say no more than two to three minutes each time (maximum 40–50 words at each stage), 20–30 minutes in total, until you have reached the end.

1 *Think about the occupation/profession you have chosen from the above list. Imagine a person fulfilling this role and living in the special world of the genre. What is their name and what do they look like? Write a brief description in no more than 50 words. WRITE.*

2 *They eat something. WRITE.*

3 *They drink. WRITE.*

4 *They meet someone. WRITE.*

5 *They get dressed (or undressed). WRITE.*

6 *They travel somewhere. WRITE.*

7 *They witness something amazing. WRITE.*

8 *They have an accident, or witness one. WRITE.*

9 *They chase what appears to be a woman or a man. WRITE.*

10 *They make an excited phone call or write a letter. WRITE.*

11 *They confront someone or something. WRITE.*

12 *They fall ill or nearly die. WRITE.*

13 *They are rescued by another character from the special world (choose one from the above). WRITE.*

14 *Bring the story to a conclusion. WRITE.*

Read over what you have written. Is there any basis in it for a story you can develop? It may not initially be coherent; maybe some of the connections are more like jumps, but do not dismiss them too easily. It can be a mistake to try to tie everything up neatly. Sometimes gaps and jumps in action can point the way to a more interesting storyline. Play around with it, see if you can make it work or if it feeds into anything you are already writing.

The demands of genre

The interrelation between plot and character is fundamentally important in creative writing. Getting the balance right between character and plot is one of the crucial achievements of successful writing. Achieving this balance and finding the answers to plot problems often come back to genre, and the plot and character needs are often genre specific. In certain forms of writing you want easily understood characters; anything too deep and three-dimensional would slow the story down and work against it. It is like having a brake on the narrative. Other stories, less fast-paced stories, cry out for fully realized, rounded and developed characters and therefore slower plots, plots that allow the characters to breathe and the character relationships to be more than paper-thin.

Characters in murder mysteries may be functional, may not 'leap off the page', but it is not to say that they are 'bad'. It is rather a question of the needs of the story. What did the writer want us to see and experience, what genre were they writing in? Remember what we said about 'flat' and 'round' characters and the need for both. Having fully developed and three-dimensional characters might work against the needs of a fast-paced, hard-boiled detective story or thriller because it would slow down the story too much. It would be against the demands of the genre. The demands of the genre are that characters are thinner and more two-dimensional because this helps the story move along; it helps the plot.

The demands of genre exert a huge influence on every aspect of a piece of creative work. A work in one genre or another will set up expectations in readers, expectations that have to be met, or if you want to take on and test and expand the parameters the genre, challenged successfully. One of the biggest decisions you can take as a writer is to decide what genre you want to write in. To a degree, it dictates much of what follows for you in your writing and in your career.

Publishers like books that fall into genres. They need to know when they publish something if it is horror, romance, science fiction, literary fiction or whatever. Film companies feel the same. It helps them to pigeonhole and to market the product to the right audience. It is reasonable advice when you are starting out not to write across genres or mix genres, because such a book, though perhaps incredibly inventive and even groundbreaking, might find it hard to secure a publisher. The fact that publishers say they are always looking for the next new thing does not mean that they will be able to recognize it when it turns up. Finding the right area to work in can take an age. It is one of the major decisions of the writer. Different genres have different demands and working within those genres means you take on those demands because they shape and inform the work you produce.

How to let characters go

We have spent a lot of time in this book trying to get characters to come to life. Characters *do* take on lives of their own. It is what writers want to happen most of all, but the other side of it is that we have to say goodbye to them. Both writers and readers have to say goodbye to characters and their worlds and when they have come vividly to life, it is not always easy. Some characters take such a very real, strong public life that the public don't want to let them go. Fans of Dickens' Little Nell, a character in *The Old Curiosity Shop* were reported to have rushed to ships arriving in New York harbour and called out to the sailors, who may have had the chance to read the final instalment, 'Is Little Nell still alive?' The more recent phenomenon of Harry Potter clearly shows how a character and a world can capture the public imagination and even become public property. For a writer this must be a wonderful thing but it can also present problems. With a hungry public demanding more and more of the character it can become hard to keep up with the sheer writing, even if you want to. And then if you want to stop writing them and say goodbye, the public may find that difficult to accept.

Case Study: The case of Sherlock Holmes

The age in which Sherlock Holmes was created was a time when faith and belief in authority was weakening; people had many questions and Holmes was a character with answers. He could solve puzzling cases by reasoning, by application of the new powerful methodology of science. This appealed to readers in the troubled late nineteenth and early twentieth centuries. It still appeals as his fame in book, TV and film testifies. HOLMES is the name of the Home Office Large Major Enquiry System, used by UK Police Forces from 1986 in major incidents like serial murders, multi-million pound fraud cases and major disasters.

Holmes came to be much more than the consulting detective from a few crime stories; he quickly came to stand for something much bigger than a mere fictional character, but this became a problem for Conan Doyle. Tired of writing the Sherlock Holmes stories, Doyle wanted to concentrate on his other writing, from which he felt he was being distracted. He wrote to his mother that he must 'save my mind for better things'. It also annoyed him that people were confusing the author with his creation, something which he wrote about in a poem in reply to 'an undiscerning critic' in which he wrote that the 'doll' (Holmes) and its maker (Conan Doyle) were not identical. Having had enough, Conan Doyle decided to kill Holmes off and he did it in a story called *The Final Problem* published in *The Strand Magazine* in 1893. Holmes fought with his arch enemy Moriarty, and they both famously fell over the Reichenbach Falls. Watson witnessed it and as usual wrote about it. But Holmes' public were very unhappy. 'Save Holmes' societies sprang up. People marched on the offices of *The Strand Magazine* in London. The character of Sherlock Holmes had grown too strong to be killed off and eventually the author had to relent and bring Holmes back to life, which he did in *The Hound of the Baskervilles*, first published in 1902. The advance from the publishers no doubt helped sway Doyle too, but once he was back, Holmes was with Doyle forever. He had become stamped on the public consciousness and he remains with us to this day, vigorous and strong in ever new adaptations. Conan Doyle strongly felt the need to kill Holmes off but as we have seen, his public would not let him. J. K. Rowling has had to judge the right time to end the series of Harry Potter books. Those are decisions that the majority of writers may not ever have to make but in terms of saying goodbye and letting a character go, all writers are faced with an equally difficult bereavement.

Letting go of your writing

Bringing a character to life is the most wonderful achievement for a writer. You can come to love their life and spending time in their company, but there is another important part of writing that we have to deal with as writers, and that is how to let them go. Creating character is breathing fire into them, fire and life; breathing air into their months and nostrils, feeling it in their lungs, sensing it activating their arms, legs and thoughts. When your characters begin to think and feel and breathe and want and desire and need and cry and love like a real person, then they are truly alive. But how do you say goodbye to character with such life and love and drive and energy?

We are faced with letting our work go in so many ways; if you are in a writer's group you have to present it for the criticism of your peers. In the professional world, we have to let a manuscript go to agents or publishers and editors. If writing scripts, we have to let them go and get into the hands of producers, directors and actors. Letting go of your writing can be hard for a writer and not enough is said on this matter. All the teaching about writing is geared to helping writers produce the work in the first place. The topics covered are often how to start, where to get ideas from, how to overcome writer's block, how to keep on writing through the middle part, and so on, but there is also the question of how you finish and what you do with the piece then. This is not the issue of how you get it published or performed; that is something important that is well covered in many books on creative writing. This is another issue around finishing too. It is not easy when you have invested time, energy, imagination, hard work and money and brought your book or script to life to be faced with the fact of no longer writing it. You spend so much time with a piece of work, you breathe life into it, which itself is some sort of miracle, you set it up on its legs, see it take its first few steps, then get stronger and stronger till in the end it runs vigorously away from you into the waiting arms of the world (to suffer acclaim or bitter rejection), that you can be lost without it. Letting it go is hard.

Bringing a character to life can be magical; you put so much energy and life as a writer into the character that you can reach the stage where you don't want to say goodbye to them at all, that you want to keep writing them. When you create a world and the characters in that world come to life, it can be fun to go there every day and write for them and see what they are saying now. It can be such fun that you do not want to stop. You love them and their world so much that saying goodbye can seem impossible. It can also seem easier to stay in this world you have created than to create a new world with all is attendant pains of creating and giving birth. It is a comfortable place: somewhere good to stay. This feeling must be akin to that of an actor inhabiting the role so much that he becomes that character on and off stage or set. Jeremy Brett inhabited the character of Sherlock Holmes so fully in the television series that he had difficulty separating himself from it.

So, when you finish a piece you can be sad because you realize you will no longer be engaged on that project, spending time in the company of the people you have created, living in their world, knowing their lives as your own (knowing their lives better than your own sometimes). To live your life with characters in a magical, imaginary world you have created can be such a wonderful thing that leaving it can give you a feeling of being bereft. To have a play in development means it is written and is being rehearsed by actors and director. As a writer you can do no more to it. You have to let it go and let the director and actors do their job and realize the script, most probably in ways you did not dream of. That is one form of goodbye where the characters in your script are going on to another existence, hopefully a rich, fulfilling, rounded one. But whether it is a play, novel or film script, you as the writer are faced with an empty desk, an empty page, and empty world because those characters that you have come to love are no longer in it and you are no longer in their world. You can miss these characters even as you try to go through the process again, picking up the reins of another set of characters in another play or story you want to write. Losing the characters from the energized world in your head and heart can feel like a sort of grief and even a betrayal. You can feel that you don't want to start again with new people and it can be difficult to do so. These emotions can feed into you not knowing what to write next. The best thing is to start again. Get back on the horse. You will begin to feel the pulse of new lives as they come too and you can work with hope that life will burn as brightly in them as with the other characters in the world that you have left behind.

A good way of getting round this loss is to try to have something 'on the go'. If you are always writing something, you have to worry less about what you are leaving behind and how to start something new. If you get stuck with a piece of writing, or tired of it, or need to give it a rest, you can just switch to another project or begin writing another part of the same project. If you are stuck on chapter three, start writing chapter four, or five or six. Don't *allow* yourself to get stuck. If you can have two or three things coming along at the same time, it avoids the questions 'How do I start? And how do I stop writing this piece?' These are the sorts of questions that can lead to a devil of procrastination. Do not worry about finishing *or* starting. If you are always writing something, even if it is in your notebook, then you do not have that terrible thought of how to begin or how not to end; you can let something go that's hanging over you.

Case Study: Roualt

Whether it is true or not, there is a moral in a story about the painter Georges Roualt. Like a lot of creative artists, he did not like to part with his work, but like all artists there were bills to pay. On one occasion someone who had bought a painting from him took it back to him and asked him to repair a small chip. Roualt did not, could not, stop at the repair but began to repaint the whole painting, so much so that the owner had to rush back and seize it off him again for fear of losing the work of art he had originally bought. Roualt could not stop; the creator in him wanted to carry on living with the object, inhabiting it, living in that world. But we have to let go of our characters and of the world we create. We cannot keep tinkering. There is such a thing as writing and writing over a manuscript and ruining it.

10 TIPS FOR SUCCESS

1 *Learn from other writers.*

2 *It is not only helpful to look at your own writing to help yourself to learn, but essential to look at what other writers have done.*

3 *Each genre has a special world with rules and characteristics. You must use them if you are writing in a particular genre.*

4 *Don't mix genres, especially when you are starting out.*

5 *The interrelation between plot and character is fundamentally important. Getting the balance right between character and plot is one of the crucial achievements of successful writing.*

6 *We need 'flat' and 'round' characters, depending on the needs of the plot.*

7 *Your writing should never be the object of its own interest.*

8 *Your characters will tell you when they have come to life.*

9 *One of the hardest parts of writing is to let go of your characters and say goodbye.*

10 *Having several things 'on the go' can be a good way of keeping writing.*

12

A few final words – further work

In writing there is no story that, with a bit of work, can't be made better or more readable, with stronger characters or a more interesting and better plot.

Now you are coming to the end of this book, you should know the answers to such questions as these:

- Do you write strong plots but weak characters?
- Do you need to find ways of strengthening your characters without diluting the plot?
- Are your plots full of pace, tight and intricate but do you have cardboard characters?
- Do you understand something of the relationship between character and plot?
- Are you equally good at characters and plot?

If you answered yes to the last question, then you could well have banked huge amounts of money because books and films with strong characters and a good story are the kinds of books and films audiences queue up for and, if audiences queue up, publishers and producers will too. But for those who still need help with either character or plot, or both, there will hopefully have been something for you in this book. And hopefully now you can go on to put what you have learned into effect and to practise more. Never stop practising.

Writing in and out of your comfort zone

After reflecting on yourself and your methods throughout this book, you should know how you go about your writing and be able to identify your strengths and weaknesses. Now ask yourself what you could do to develop both the area that you are good at and that motivates you (your strength) and the area that seems less important to you or what you are less good at (your weakness). For instance, if plot is secondary to character for you, if you make strong plots but weak characters, or strong characters but weak plots, think about how you can improve the area you are weakest in.

We often make the mistake of practising what we are good at or what motivates us, partly because it is easier. But because we are doing something well, we can convince ourselves that by doing it over and over we are doing all right. Not only that, but we can believe that we are practising and improving. Yes, we are practising what we are good at, but what about what we are less good at?

Does it not make sense to spend more time on what we are less good at than to stay in our comfort zone? By going over and over what we can already do well we may be consolidating our skills, and that is important, but the parts we are not good at wither and fall away. If you challenge yourself, you will develop your repertoire. Moving out of your comfort zone is also an important part of developing in any field. If a golfer who was a good driver of the ball never practised his short game, his putts and chips around the green, it would be reasonable to expect his short game to let him down when it was most needed. Gary Player said, when called a lucky golfer, 'Yes, the more I practise the luckier I get.' Practise your writing; write, write, write, in all areas. The more you practice, the luckier you will get.

Key Idea

We can improve more by focusing on what we cannot do well rather than what we can do well.

Revision

Revision is another word that beginning writers fear. They fear it because they do not know how to revise. They do not have the skills or the developed sense of judgement to know what works and what does not work. Such judgement comes over time, through making many mistakes and finding ways around them.

Do not be afraid of revision. Do not be afraid to try things out. The real writing is *rewriting*. Do not be afraid to move things around: words, sentences, whole sections. Learning what to cut and what to leave is a judgement that comes over time. Think of your writing as live and organic. Taking a bit out and putting it somewhere else will not kill it, but could well give it a new life and form. Pruning roses makes them grow again, harder and better; writing is the same.

W. H. Auden once said that poems were not finished, they were abandoned. Perhaps it is true of all writing. We all have to learn to stop and let go. Letting go is hard but there is only one piece of advice to give here. When you come to the end, stop.

You make a character real through:

1 *Their name.*

2 *Description – outer things: what they look like, what they wear.*

3 *Setting – where they belong, where they live, their office, their environment and how this affects them.*

4 *Inner life – their motives, desires, wants and needs: if there is something significant that they must have.*

5 *Actions – what they do to get what they want.*

6 *Dialogue – what they say to get what they want.*

7 *What others say about them and do to them.*

8 *Obstacles to what they want – what they have to overcome.*

9 *Opposition to what they want – people or things they have to overcome.*

10 *Their relationship to other characters in the story.*

Appendix one

On coming outside, talking fast a young man sneezed twice, loud
explosions, then walked on. Sun lit up the beautiful droplet drift.
I moved on, fast.

The notes start with 'on coming outside'. This tells us that, as the
reader, we are with the viewpoint figure, the one making the notes.
We are outside and the young man who in a few words is going to
sneeze was inside and has just come outside. 'On coming outside';
what sort of writing is this? Perhaps a more conversational 'coming
outside' or 'stepping outside' might be better. But it really could
be described as functional writing. It does the needful; it gets us
going and begins to tell us where we are. It is like those little steps
someone on a toboggan might make to get going before they leap
aboard and build up speed, or that a sprinter might make at the
start of a race. In that way, the little steps 'on coming outside' do a
job, but in other ways they are inconsequential, empty. The phrase
says what it says but no more. Can these little steps be used to get
started be any better? Surely a sprinter needs to get away in the best
possible way. A poor start can mean a poor race.

'On coming outside' has the feeling of scaffolding about it. It gives
nothing but the most general context. It tells us someone who was
inside has come outside, but inside what, a tent, a palace, an office?
And come out into what, a field, a park, a street? To find more out
we would need more words to follow that tell us where he was and
what he has come outside into. But instead of just adding more
words and telling the reader where exactly outside was, can we find
another way that also gets us going but which says more?

Can we find something else, something to replace the scaffolding?
Ultimately we are asking if we can get the words we write to work
on more than one level. It would help you to know that the notes
were made on a California University campus and the young man
was a student. Would you know that from the initial notes and
does it matter? Well, the writer knows it so how would he show
it? Suppose he takes out 'On coming outside' and replaces it with
'leaving class' so that we now get:

Leaving class, talking fast, a young man sneezed twice.

'Leaving class' is a gain because it gives us a more specific
context. There is a suggestion of a classroom or of an educational
establishment, though it does not explicitly say it. As sometimes
happens when we change words, we lose something; we no longer

know that he is coming outside though we do know that he is leaving one place and going to another. He is leaving class so he is going from one room to another, either into a corridor or going outside and as we will see later, we can understand that he is outside from the rest of the piece. Though again it does not say it explicitly, 'leaving class' begins to suggest something about character. This is a student, or perhaps a teacher; probably a student because he is a young man. What you need to decide when you are working like this is, is the gain of the change greater than the loss?

What else do we know about the young man after making this change? We know he is talking fast and probably that he comes out fast. What is he talking fast about? He might be talking about his rent but it is possible that he has been engaged in the subject of the class, that he is involved in his studies. He is leaving class, so let's assume he is talking fast about his class. He comes out of class, talking fast, he sneezes. We are learning more about him as a character but what about these sneezes? The piece now reads:

> Leaving class, talking fast a young man sneezed twice, loud explosions; then walked on. Sun lit up the beautiful droplet drift. I moved on, fast.

We have more of a context. We are in or close to an educational establishment of some sort. He has left class clearly excited. He sneezes and either he does not care to cover his nose or does not have time as he sneezes because these are loud explosions. The sneezing does not register with him. What does this way of sneezing tell us about the character of this young man? Most people feel the need to cover their nose when they sneeze either with their hand or a tissue; it is basic politeness. But this young man does not, either because he is so excited about what he is talking about or because he just does not. What he is talking about is clearly more important to him and the sneezes are just sneezes. What's the problem? He is out of class; he wants to sneeze, so he sneezes. The sneezes shoot from him in loud explosions sending a shower of germs into the air. His lack of consideration of others is implied. This is what caught the eye of the watching writer.

By changing the beginning we have started better and focused the writing a little more on its subject. Let's see if we can focus it some more.

> The young man rushes outside from class, talking fast he sneezes, twice.

It is important to keep in that he sneezed twice, not just because he did, but because, while one sneeze might be excused, two looks like carelessness, or rudeness. We will also go on to show that it is good to keep in that they are explosions because that shows he did not try and muffle them with hand or tissue but do we need to keep 'loud' or 'in the air?' Surely both are implied. Explosions are loud and where else would the sneeze end up but in the air? And if it is not quite implied yet, as soon as we see the droplet-drift in sunlight it has to be in air, so here are other bits of *explanation*, other pieces of scaffolding that we can leave out.

Two further changes can help focus the piece of writing even more. Simply switching 'walked on' for 'talked on' makes this little phrase less ordinary and obvious and could add to this sense of his conversation being more important to him than social etiquette. It is a nice joke for the author to want to rush out of the way of the droplet drift for fear of catching whatever virus the young man has just ejected into the atmosphere, but the use of the 'I' also means the author intrudes. The young man is the subject of the piece, maybe it is better if the piece focuses on him and removing the author from the last line will also help focus on the character and the incident. These changes result in this:

> *Leaving class, talking fast a young man sneezed twice, (loud) explosions; then talked on. Sun lit up the beautiful droplet drift; every one.*

'Loud' is bracketed here because the writer knows it needs to come out but can't think what to put in its place. The rhythm just does not seem to work without something there. But removing the writer from the end and substituting 'every one' focuses very much on the droplet drift. The piece comes to rest on these words 'every one' like music coming down to the last chord and letting it fade away. If it were a camera shot, the camera would be held there on the droplets picked out by the sun, all the drops, every one. The words 'every one' have such connotations for the rest of the piece too. They are intended to mean all the drops but they could do extra work and mean all his arguments too. He is so enthusiastic and idealistic and excited about what he is learning that he wants to spray these ideas around the world, every one. Maybe his arguments will also infect everyone. This is a good example of one change doing a lot more work than just one task.

Here is another version with some further alterations. Can you spot them? In the piece now we see that the young man is careless. Lost in the excitement of his studies and his world, he sneezes twice and does not worry about anyone else catching his cold. He does not make any attempt to cover up his nose, he does not worry about possibly infecting many others; all of this tells us about his character.

Leaving class talking fast, a young student sneezes twice – two explosions. Sunlight shows the beautiful droplet-drift shoot from his nose.

'Loud' has now been removed and 'two' added in its place. 'Two' is one syllable also and therefore keeps the rhythm. The writer did worry about the repetition of 'two' immediately following 'twice' but thought this actually emphasized that the young man did it twice, he sneezed twice, as if once wasn't bad enough. This actually added to the sense that it was something noteworthy and potentially revealing of character. Did you notice also that there has been a change in tense here? The writer has now changed *sneezed* for *sneezes*. He did this to bring the piece into the present tense, to make it happen now in front of us. He has also changed the ending and taken out the words 'every one' even though he quite liked it. Why? Because, on reflection, saying 'sun lit up the beautiful droplet drift; every one' is inaccurate. The droplet drift is one entire thing, it is a singular drift; there are not several droplet-drifts. The words 'every one' were intended to show the sunlight picking out each individual droplet in the drift, every one but this cannot work in this construction so it had to go. Showing instead the droplet-drift 'shoot from his nose' adds to the image of the droplets shooting out into the air.

Is the writer happy now? Not yet. Look this version over again.

Leaving class talking fast, a young student sneezes twice – two explosions. Sunlight shows the beautiful droplet-drift shoot from his nose.

You may decide this is or isn't better than the first revised version. That does not matter. This exercise has in the main been about illustrating a process, a process often called 'worrying over' or, if this feels too negative, polishing a piece to try to improve it. Whether you believe it has been improved or not does not matter. But the piece is now more focused on the incident.

'RE-VISION'

In revision, always go back to the *vision* of the piece – what the piece is about. Revision is a re-vision, another look at it. Let's have one more go at revising the lines we were polishing. This is how we left it:

Leaving class talking fast, a young student sneezes twice – two explosions. Sunlight shows the beautiful droplet-drift shoot from his nose.

At its core, the piece we have been revising is about a sneeze. The piece is written by someone from another cold, more northern country where cold germs are mostly unseen. What has interested the writer here is that in California, this different part of the world, the normally invisible sneeze has been made visible by the sunlight. The writer can see the droplet drift happen in sunlight and he has found this wet droplet shower beautiful. This piece is about the moment of marvelling at the quality of light that will reveal a normally invisible sneeze. This could be the focus of another revision.

> *Leaving class talking fast, a young student sneezes twice – loud explosions. Clear sunlight shows the golden droplet-drift shoot from his nose.*

'Clear sunlight' aims at showing the clarity of light. Why has the writer taken out the word beautiful and replaced it with golden, as in 'golden droplet-drift'? Because he seeks to get across the idea that it was transformed by the light into something unusual and visually striking. Have we improved it? Is this final one the best one of all the revisions or is it that each revision looks at it differently? Polishing the words has certainly resulted in a sharp, clear picture of the simple incident. Where the writer comes from, sneezes are almost always invisible but in the clear Californian sunlight the droplets shower stands out clearly. In this climate, because it is a sunny day and the quality of light is clear, the droplets are made visible to the naked eye. Caught in the light we see them shoot from him. If it is significant at all, it is because of the unusualness of it and because of the beauty of seeing the droplets in a cloud shoot out and shine in the sunlight. This is what the writer was after and what he pointed to but did not say in his notes. *That's why they were notes.* Whether this is an improvement or not, whether it hits the target aimed at, is something that different readers and writers can debate. Some might see other ways of improving it, but all of the revisions we have looked at have moved the piece on quite a way from the first few notes jotted down in the writer's notebook.

How has the piece developed, where has it gone? We now have a potential character in a potential setting that we can work with. But the real point here is that there all the scaffolding has been taken down, there is none left up and now the public can be invited to the grand opening.

Appendix two

She was standing on the wooden porch outside the café. She wore a pink and brown waterproof top and tights that were coloured in bands, pink, brown, white and cream like liquorice allsorts down her legs. She was pulling her blonde hair back from her face with her pink mittens, while watching her Mum tie the yapping dog up before going inside. The dog bounced up on his leash at a woman who came past. The woman shrank away from the mud in small black socks up his short furry legs and hanging from the undersides of his ragged fur and hurried on into the café. The girl scolded the dog and told him to stop barking. The dog stopped barking and stood looking at her, cute with his spiky biscuit-coloured hair in his eyes and tongue hanging out. The girl came into the café. The dog yapped again. The girl screwed her face up and stomped out. She had a small, mobile face that could scowl, look puzzled, thoughtful and interested one after another. She stamped one of her black sandals that had the striped stockings peeking through, pointed a finger at the dog and made a stern face, the way she'd undoubtedly seen her Mum do to her. Looking at her, the dog stopped yapping. The girl went back in. The dog yapped again. The girl opened the door. Her waterproof top, catching on the door handle, parted to reveal a pink T-shirt on which was a steaming mug of hot drink in a red cup.

'You're making him bark by going in and out,' said her Mum.

Taking it further

Egri, L., *The Art of Dramatic Writing* (New York: Touchstone, 1946).

Frey, J. N., *How to Write a Damn Good Novel* (London: Papermac, 1987).

King, S., *On Writing* (London: Hodder & Stoughton, 2000).

Lukeman, N., *The Plot Thickens* (London: Hale, 2002).

Scott Card, O. et al, *How to Write a Million* (London: Robinson Books, 1995).

Stein, S., *Solutions for Writers* (London: Souvenir Press, 1998).

Index